Where's Heidi?

One Sister's Journey

Lisa M. Buske

WHERE'S HEIDI?
ONE SISTER'S JOURNEY

Lisa M. Buske

http://LisaMBuske.com
Email: lbuskewriter@aol.com

Cover photograph taken by Lisa M. Buske

Scriptures taken from the Holy Bible, New International Version®, NIV®. Copyright © 1973, 1978, 1984, 2011 by Biblica, Inc.™ Used by permission of Zondervan. All rights reserved worldwide. www.zondervan.com The "NIV" and "New International Version" are trademarks registered in the United States Patent and Trademark Office by Biblica, Inc.™

ISBN 978-0615683607

Library of Congress Control Number: 2013902060

To Read Reviews:

Dedication

For the sibling grieving the loss of their brother or sister ~ This is my story of God's love, provision, and constant care during a time when I didn't think He even knew I was alive. This book is for you. May you be inspired, motivated, and hopeful as you reflect on the difficult days of past in anticipation of the days ahead.

For the parents of our missing persons ~ I pray my story will help you to relate with your surviving children. May you understand our grief is as deep as yours is, although on a different scope. We are the siblings.

For our community and the many volunteers ~ Without your time, dedication, and love we could not have survived those first hours, days, and months. You were angels in disguise and we are forever grateful for each of you. With much love and emotion, I say thank you.

A COVER WITH MEANING

Heidi picture isn't on the cover. I wrote *Where's Heidi? One Sister's Journey* was to let others know there is hope after loss. My loss is the result of kidnapping. Yours may be completely different or the same than you realize. Everyone experiences loss at some point. This is why I didn't use Heidi's photograph on the cover.

The idea of Heidi's face displayed on the cover like yet another missing person's flyer tore at my heart. My desire is to help others, not just my family and community. I felt her smile might limit your ability to personalize this story as your own.

After much prayer, this photograph taken at the location of my sister's disappearance came to be. I pray you understand and appreciate the thought that went into this decision.

The cover represents hope, community, remembrance, and God's working in my life. A photograph of my beautiful sister, Heidi M. Allen, only captures the *remembrance*.

~ 1 ~

The Significance of Each:

Hope: April 3, 2011 ~ I faced the most difficult anniversary associated with my sister's kidnapping. I struggled to accept the fact of Heidi's mirrored years on earth and in heaven. In the midst of my pain, a rose bloomed on this very same day, in the garden dedicated to her, God's reminder for all of us to never, give up.

Community: The rose of hope is in the *Heidi Allen Remembrance Garden,* in front of the same convenience store where Heidi disappeared. This *remembrance garden* exists because our community functions as a large family. When the going gets tough, we pull together. What better way to thank them and illustrate a sense of community than with the very garden they dedicated to Heidi.

Remembrance: The store in the background is a constant reminder of Heidi's kidnapping. I will never forget my sister and neither will our community. The building represents the day our town changed, rallied, and united in spite of great tragedy.

God's working in my life: Transformation is in God's time. There are many things I took for granted or glanced over in the past. God showed me they were blessings in disguise. I am the woman I am today because of the journey following my sister's abduction. Instead of viewing the location of your tragedy as negative, let it fade into the background and focus on the hope in front of you.

Only God could bloom a rose on the very day, 18 years prior, that it snowed. A bleeding heart encouraged my hurting one.

Praise be to the God and Father of our Lord Jesus Christ,

the Father of compassion and the God of all comfort,

who comforts us in all our troubles,

so that we can comfort those in any trouble

with the comfort we ourselves have received from God.

2 Corinthians 1:3-4

TABLE OF CONTENTS

For Heidi…
I love you, baby sister!

Where's Heidi? One Sister's Journey is a book written by Lisa M. Buske, our oldest daughter, about the abduction of her younger sister, Heidi M. Allen. It's a true account of her struggles, of losing and regaining her faith.

This book is very personal and moving to us as her parents. We lost our daughter, Heidi, and we worried about losing our other daughter, Lisa, because of this tragedy. This book is a testament to how she saved herself through this journey.

Her courage to write this book in order to help others has made our hearts full.

With love and respect for all Lisa has done,

Ken and Sue Allen
Parents to both Heidi and Lisa

PREFACE

Where's Heidi? One sister's Journey, first drafted in September 2006 as an entry for a writing contest, developed into my firsthand account of being the sister to one of America's missing persons. My first draft was sixty-two pages of emotional vomit. With time, prayer, mentoring, and a Faithful God, you now hold this book of hope in your hands.

My only and younger sister, Heidi M. Allen, was kidnapped while working alone at the *D & W Convenience Store* in New Haven, New York. She remains missing today.

To write this book meant I needed to remember those first hours, days, months, and years as if they were today. It was a painful and difficult process yet it was important to relive it so others, like you, can know there is hope in spite of life's tragedies.

I want this book to illustrate, to the best of my memory, how Heidi's kidnapping affected my life. Much of 1994 is lost, just like my sister. People, dates, and timing are to the best of my human and grief-stricken memory.

I asked questions of family (who share a similar memory loss), read most of the newspaper articles cut so many years ago, and prayed for God to guide each word.

It is my hope and prayer to share the impact of Heidi's kidnapping accurately. I have learned my memory isn't something I can trust. Although my brain struggles to remember, please know I write and share with the purest of intentions, and to my best recollection.

Grief and tragedy have the power to hold you and your thoughts hostage.

Thankfully, God has the power to restore clarity and hope for the lost.

When Heidi disappeared, attended Saturday evening mass with my Gram and Aunt Nancy. I didn't have a personal relationship with Jesus and I don't know if Heidi did or not. I can only pray she did.

After Heidi's kidnapping, the closest I came to church were the numerous candlelight vigils held in Heidi's honor. Church, God, and prayer were not a part of my life.

One candlelight vigil represents my breaking point. Instead of leaning on God for support, I ran in the opposite direction fueled with anger and grief for fuel. I wanted no part in a God who first tore my sister from our lives and then forgot about me. Of course, this was a misunderstanding on my part but the years to follow spiraled into some of the darkest days in my life.

Thankfully, one child ignited the flame necessary to illuminate my confusion and introduce me to the Only One who could heal the hurt: Jesus Christ.

I pray you read this book and understand it is possible to survive after the loss of a loved one. Fear, anger, and grief are not to be our life's focus but instead love and hope should be our goal.

ACKNOWLEDGMENTS

First, I want to thank God for sending His One and Only Son, Jesus Christ ~ It is only through my relationship with Him that I am able to write this book.

My husband, Ed, and our daughter, Mary ~ your love & support through this entire process are a blessing. Thanks for always being there, I love you both!!

My parents ~ your strength, encouragement, and constant love are priceless gifts.

My friends and family ~ your love and prayers encourage me daily.

To Alyssa ~ for editing this book.

To Vie Herlocker and Elaine W. Miller ~ I covet your love, encouragement, and prayers as you mentor me to be the best woman, author, & speaker for God.

Beth and M.J. ~ your prayers, mentoring, and friendship bring a smile to my face.

A special thanks to my writers' critique group ~ Amy, Diane, Elaine, Jody, Mary, Melissa, and Paula. Your honest critiques encourage and inspire me.

For those I have not named personally ~ you continue to be pillars of strength, support, and joy in my life. You might be ever so silent in the background but your love and friendships are priceless treasures. To list you all would fill a book.

To those who have and continue to pray for Heidi, my family, and the publication of this first book ~ your faith and heart for Heidi are precious blessings in our lives. Thank you.

INTRODUCTION

A time to be born
And a time to die...
Ecclesiastes 3:2a

On April 3, 1994, my only sister, Heidi M. Allen was abducted from the *D & W Convenience store.* It was Easter Sunday. My life changed the moment I heard my aunt's voice on the answering machine. She called to notify me. I spent years in search of something or someone to fill the void.

The most obvious search was, and is, for Heidi. I never fathomed a kidnapping would happen in my hometown, or that my sister would be the one to make the history books in Oswego County, New York.

In my search for someone who understood how I felt, I visited libraries and various search engines. The result was the same: nothing. Yes, there are books written for the parents, grandparents, or generalized books, but nothing written specifically for the sister.

A parent's grief and emotional state are the priority when a child goes missing. The remaining siblings experience a similar range of emotions due to the loss of their brother or sister. We grieve, get angry, and the slew of emotions in between, but for the most part we set these aside to be there for our parents. It is what we must do. Our parents do not need one more thing to worry about.

This book is the result of my empty searching. In 2010 I prepared my first book proposal. I found a book written by another grieving sister. Karen Beaudin's *A Child is Missing* details how her sister's kidnapping affected her life both as a child and then as an adult. I devoured this book and contacted Karen immediately. Her book was an answer to my prayer and our friendship was a blessing as I continued to revise and finish this book.

I write so others who grieve the loss of their sibling will know it is okay to be sad, angry, and grieve the loss of their brother or sister. It is normal and necessary. In the writing of *Where's Heidi? One Sister's Journey*, I learned how powerful the sting of grief is on one's family and their minds. I want this book to be the best representation of my thoughts and actions from the moment Heidi disappeared until the present day.

Regardless of how hard I try to remember, a majority of 1994 and 1995 are lost just like Heidi. "Mom, how can I write an honest account of those first years after Heidi's kidnapping, if I can't even remember how I transitioned from the store to the fire hall?"

"I don't know. Why don't you pray about it?"

"Good idea."

The next day God answered this prayer while Mom and I sorted through dusty boxes from storage. Sneezes, tears, and laughter shared between mother and daughter. Our goal to find something to help me remember was a success and our bond strengthened. Hours into our mental travels back in time, we discovered a treasure.

Mom's words and excitement startle me and cause me to stop. "Found it!"

I didn't know we were looking for anything in particular, but obviously, she was.

A priceless gift only God could have provided, just when I needed it. Within one of the plastic totes was an orange folder labeled: "Chronology of the Heidi Allen Case: April 3, 1994".

"This occupied you for days. You were so proud of yourself when you finished. Not to mention, so were we. This should help you with the book."

In the left pocket of the folder was a typed list of every clipped newspaper article from April 3, 1994 through June 4, 1995. It included the date, newspaper name, journalist's name and its headline. As if this was not enough, hole punched in the center was a timeline from the minute Heidi disappeared through October 28, 1995.

On the right hand side was one of the "Memory Books" put together by volunteers. Photocopies of articles, notes, and photographs fill the pages. God knew then I would need something to help me remember. My busy work served as my memory when the time came years later. I didn't recall a plan, "I'm going to write a book one day so I'll sit at the computer and organize these newspaper articles and chain of events." Thankfully, God did.

Getting Through

One never gets over the loss of their sibling or child. The unread newspaper articles and saved news stories serve as my memory for at least the initial six months following Heidi's kidnapping. Some events remain etched on my brain, but the majority, lost with my sister. Grief has the power and potential to take your mind captive.

I want to remember but something prevents it. What am I missing? Is my lack of memory God's way to protect me? Will I ever remember it all? On the other hand, do I really want to? Questions flooded my brain.

Friends got married, neighbors passed away, and the world continued to spin on its axis. *America's Most Wanted* and *Day One* both broadcast Heidi's case. A $20,000 reward offered. Benefits held across the county. A search and rescue expert from the *Heidi Search Center* in San Antonio, Texas even joined the efforts. The National Guard joined the search. Life continued. The only thing I could focus on was, "Heidi is missing", and I was not sure how to live without her.

We need to trust God during the storm so we can use what He has given us as a sail to make it across the ocean of trials. When forced to anchor in tough weather, we need to trust God so we do not sink. Life with a loved one missing can make living an ongoing storm. Sadly, I wouldn't let myself trust God at that point in my life.

PROLOGUE

I stirred awake when I heard the answering machine.

"Heidi is missing!" Aunt Nancy yelled into the phone. "Heidi has been kidnapped."

I sat bolt upright as her voice echoed through the cottage. "Your parents need you at the store. Get there NOW." Click...

Oh my gosh. This can't be true. "There has to be a mistake." Then the adrenaline and nerves started. Within moments, my husband was awake, dressed and driving me to the *D & W Convenience store* only three miles away.

Law enforcement, yellow tape, and flashing lights greeted us.

I could not breathe. I felt weak. It was real. Heidi WAS missing.

This was the end to my life as I knew it and the beginning of my lifelong quest: Where's Heidi?

CHAPTER 1

There is a time for everything...
Ecclesiastes 3:1a

The day started like Easter Sunday did in other small American towns. Heidi arrived at work early, anticipating the time she would spend with family and friends later in the afternoon. She volunteered to cover the morning shift so a coworker could spend the holiday with her children, even though it meant she would be the only one working at the store.

For a majority of the United States of America, Easter Sunday is a time of reflection, celebration, and worship honoring the resurrection of Jesus Christ. In the small town of New Haven in northern New York, people prepared for the day's events. Mothers organized breakfasts and last minute details while fathers completed their honey-do-lists before the children awakened and it was time to leave for church. While the adults scurried around in pre-dawn activity, children dreamed of their Easter baskets, egg hunts, and going to Grandma's house.

Heidi Allen was eighteen years old and worked at the local convenience store full-time to pay her way through college. She attended the same high school as me, Bishop Cunningham Jr. /Sr. High

School, a private Catholic school located in Oswego until it closed due to declining enrollment and rising costs. Heidi had a choice to make: return to public school or apply for college a year early at the conclusion of her junior year.

In 1993, Heidi applied for early admissions to Onondaga Community College. Her acceptance allowed her to complete her senior year of high school and her first year of college simultaneously. Through hard work, she earned honors and her high school diploma.

Heidi was my younger sister. I was so proud of her strong will and determination to succeed. Heidi proved she could do anything she put her mind to. She dedicated the necessary time for full-time college a year early while working full-time to pay her own tuition. She also volunteered at the Academy Street Elementary school in the Mexico Academy and Central school district.

Weekly she assisted with *Banana Splits*, a program designed to help children affected by divorce. Heidi would say that even though she was busy with school and work, the children needed to know there were people other than their families that cared. She finished with a new perspective and understanding for the needs of others, especially the children in her community.

At 5 a.m. on April 3, 1994, Heidi opened up the *D & W Convenience Store*, located at the intersection of State Route 104 and State Route 104B, and her boyfriend Brett came along to keep her company until the store got busy. Brett often accompanied her on those early mornings.

Brett left the store around 7:15 a.m., knowing his beautiful girlfriend opened up safely with customers coming in. They planned to meet later in the afternoon to deliver Easter baskets for his nieces and nephews.

In less than three hours from opening the store, all plans and agendas changed. Heidi's last known transaction registered at 7:42 a.m. A time forever engraved on my heart and in my mind as the last moment I knew my sister was alive, well, and safe. Customers entered the store just as they did every Sunday for their papers and coffee with one exception – the clerk was missing from behind the counter.

Heidi's smiling face on a Sunday morning was common, but her absence was not. Some customers took the time to yell, inquiring of her whereabouts while others simply left their money on the counter.

Finally, one customer recognized something was awry - money was accumulating on the counter and there was no sign of the clerk. He ran outside yelling for help and flagged down the first car traveling on the road, which happened to be a sheriff's deputy. The mystery and search began.

CHAPTER 2

...and a season for every activity under heaven:
Ecclesiastes 3:1b

The phone rang early for an Easter Sunday at our home. Holidays and weekends had the potential of overtime, as others were "sick". With this thought in the back of my mind, I listened, not moving from my comfortable, warm bed.

Who would call in on Easter? Of all days. I vowed not to leave home one minute earlier than scheduled. I was determined to stay snuggled in for as long as I could. I knew the answering machine would pick up after two rings so I waited to hear who dared to disturb my Easter slumber.

It was not the nursing home calling. I wish it had been. Instead of hearing the morning supervisor's grumbling voice saying, "Lisa, can you come in early?" I heard Aunt Nancy's trembling voice. "Heidi is missing. Heidi has been kidnapped. Your parents need you at the store. Get there now!" Click.

I lay there, listening as she spoke those unbelievable words.

I could not move. *This had to be a mistake. I am closing my eyes, and going back to sleep. This is a nightmare.*

The sounds of beep...beep...beep signaled a message on the answering machine.

Once the shock wore off, I jumped from the bed so abruptly that my husband sat straight up. "What's wrong?"

I could not respond but ran to the answering machine in hopes I misunderstood. I played it over repeatedly until forced to stop.

Finally, my husband, Ed, took my hands. "Let's go. Your parents need you." Being a realist, he added, "Put on something comfy."

I didn't listen. Assuming this was a misunderstanding, I changed into my uniform so I could go to work after meeting up with my parents at the *D & W convenience store.*

Within moments, we were speeding in the car.

As the miles ticked off, I stared blankly out the window. "Certainly, this is a mistake. It has to be. Kidnappings don't happen in New Haven, New York." On and on my thoughts swirled out of control.

"Lisa." I heard my husband speak my name, his voice quavering. "You're not making sense." All the thoughts that bombarded my brain were pouring incoherently out of my mouth. My husband's voice pulled me out of the dangerous daydream I entered.

I turned to him and asked, "Do you think she went to check on Uncle Don? Aunt Judy only passed away yesterday. They live within a mile of the store. I'll bet she went to check on him while it was slow." The thought offered a glimmer of hope and I was desperate to grab it.

Ed shook his head. "No, I don't think so honey."

I looked at him with fire in my eyes. Then flashing red lights caught my attention. "Oh my gosh. It is real." My stomach tightened. My body shook and tears rolled down my cheeks.

A uniformed officer approached me. "Who are you?" he demanded. "Why are you here?" Before I could respond, someone came out of the store. "That's Heidi's sister. We need her."

I do not remember the officer's name, only that it was a man. My primary concern was to find my parents. I yearned to hear them say it was a mistake and everything would be okay but this never happened.

A sheriff's deputy escorted me to a secure area. "Do you have any photographs of Heidi with you?"

"I have a couple," I said, fumbling through my purse. "And I have more at home."

Heidi just had her senior pictures taken for her high school graduation. I had a few different poses . . . Heidi smiling . . . Heidi looking scholarly . . . Heidi looking like she could take on the world . . . In addition to the professional photos were a few snapshots. I gave one of each to the officer.

"Thank you," he said, taking the photos. "These will do for now." He turned to leave, and then said, "We might need you to go home and get more later."

My hope to see my parents after my interrogation proved to be only a hope. From one secured area to the next, fear overtook me as I waited for someone to join me. I envied the closeness others had to people. At the same time though, I didn't know what I would have said if anyone did come over.

I stood by the fuel pump close to the road, far from the store – and my parents. I watched carloads of people drive by as if nothing out of the ordinary was happening. Then again, it wasn't – in their world.

How could people go to church? Did they understand we needed their help? They could have pulled over and helped to find Heidi, didn't anyone care?

Another car crawled past the store. People craned their necks, staring at all the police cars surrounding the store. My nerves shattered. *Yes, I am Heidi's sister. Yes, I am standing here, doing nothing while you drive by. Stop staring. Stop being nosy. Go celebrate Easter with your family. If you really care, stop and keep me company.*

As the morning wore on, the weather changed from rain to snow. I began to lose touch with reality. *Oh my, it's Easter for heaven's sake. Snow? You've got to be kidding me.*

As the wet snow landed on my cheeks, which were red and damp from crying, the cool precipitation felt almost refreshing.

Grief eventually replaced the self-pity. While upset for being forced to stand in the brisk weather, I understood it was for the validity of the case. Common sense told me it was the right thing to do, but my heart only ached. If only I could shake the guilt, induced from worrying, about myself. *What kind of sister was I? God forgive me, I love her.* Heidi was missing and I didn't know what to do. I didn't want to stand here another minute; I needed to do something.

Ed joined in the search for Heidi. I didn't know where he was and I felt overwhelmed, wet, and lonely. *God, do you hear me? I'm scared and I don't want to be myself.*

While I leaned against the fuel pump, crying and wallowing in self-pity, I felt pressure around my shoulders. Someone was holding me.

I turned and looked into the tear-stained face of my cousin, Missy. Finally, a family member stood close enough to touch. Still no conversation. No words were necessary.

The sounds of law enforcement radios, cars driving by, traffic slowing, and people stopping to ask questions of the sheriff's deputies monitoring the intersection became background noise to my own thought processes. Horrific thoughts heightened my fear. *Could Heidi be in that car? That van. What if Heidi's kidnappers had the nerve to stop and inquire? What if they had Heidi in the back seat or trunk unable to signal for help because she was gagged and bound?* I needed to stop thinking but was not sure what else to do.

So I stood.

I waited.

And I longed to be with my parents.

I had questions with no answers. *Where are my parents? Are they okay?*

Then, almost on cue, Kris, one of the store's owners, appeared at my side. "Your parents are fine," she said. "They sent me to check on you." Kris hugged me and tried to assure me we would be all right. "I am so sorry," she said. As Kris bared her heart to encourage me, all I thought was, stop hugging me. Get your hands off me. If there had been a bell on the door or a camera, we might have more to go on. LEAVE ME ALONE. On the outside, I accepted her help.

I knew then, just as I know today – Kris felt terrible and blamed herself for Heidi's disappearance, yet I could not say the words I knew to be true,"It's not your fault." to comfort and reassure her. Instead, I returned to the selfish sister mode, leaving her to wallow in her own guilt. In hindsight, I pray she can forgive me for this selfishness.

After awhile, Kris drifted away. As she faded from the picture, my parents drifted in. Time and space took on a different dimension. Mom and Dad were leaving, without me. Did they know I was still there? One moment we were at the store and the next, I was walking into the *New Haven Volunteer Fire Department*, which morphed into the *Heidi Allen Command Post*. Missy was already scurrying around to help. My physical location changed. I was warm and dry but I wanted my parents, even though I understood they were doing what was necessary to help find Heidi.

I wished I could go back home, crawl into bed and start the day all over again.

I watched the day unfold as if it was a movie but I knew it was not.

It was real life.

And my little sister was missing.

CHAPTER 3

A time to weep...
Ecclesiastes 3:4a

Flash back twelve hours: Ed and I joined my parents for the evening. We ordered pizza for dinner with plans to watch a movie.

We relocated to the living room to watch a western with John Wayne after reducing the pizza to only an empty, grease-stained box. I don't recall the movie title but know he was the hero and saved the day, in typical "Duke" flare.

As my parents settled into their swivel chairs, Ed sat on the couch while I snuggled into my favorite childhood chair. We heard Brett's black Dodge Cougar pull into the driveway then Heidi's feet skipping through the kitchen.

Heidi sang, "Here Comes Peter Cottontail" in her bubbly and excited voice as she came through the kitchen.

From my perch in the brown and orange flowered armchair, I swiveled my head to watch the childlike drama unfold as Heidi emerged through the door with Brett shaking his head behind her.

Arms full of baskets and goodies swayed side to side in each hand.

I laughed until tears ran down my cheeks. "You're the tallest Easter bunny I've ever seen. So they call you Peter Cottontail now?"

Heidi nodded and curtsied, then continued her performance. I assumed the role of conductor, raising my arms and hands to lead her through the next verse. Laughter overtook us and the show ended.

Mom, Dad, Ed and Brett smiled, shaking their heads as the two of us continued to act like toddlers.

Heidi, keeping up the bunny impersonation, handed out the treats she brought for each of us. Mom and Dad's brightly colored basket was full of their favorite chocolates and marshmallow bunnies. Tucked inside was a special gift just for Dad: the April edition of the *Winston Cup Illustrated*, a NASCAR magazine.

Heidi presented Ed with a bag of assorted mini chocolate bars. She handed me a card.

"Where's my candy?" I asked in mock disappointment.

"I'm sure Ed will share with you," she retorted. Then turning to Ed, she whispered, "But you don't have to."

Ed winked at me. "You better be nice to me if you want any chocolate."

"Forget it." *I will just pick up clearance candy on Monday.*

Heidi enjoyed both joking and laughing. Ed's affectionate teasing pleased her.

All too soon, the pre-Easter frivolity ended. Heidi and Brett prepared to leave for his parents' house in the neighboring town of Mexico.

"Thanks again. Happy Easter!" Mom and Dad chorused.

"Don't work too hard tomorrow," Dad added.

Heidi smiled. "No problem, love you." She turned to leave. Before she disappeared from the living room, she turned and blew an air kiss to us all.

Unwilling for the fun to end, I pretended to pout. "What about me? No Happy Easter? First, no candy and now no holiday wishes. Hmm." But, unable to keep up the pretense, with a wink, I stood up to give her a hug.

Heidi made a motion to blow me my own kiss.

I put my hand up. "Too late…"

My parents shook their heads. "Not again."

Brett and Ed rolled their eyes. They were used to our sisterly goofiness.

Heidi laughed as she walked toward the door. "You don't NEED chocolate, you're already fat," Heidi taunted. "Besides, I gave you a card."

"I may be fat, but I can diet," I called after her. "You have a big butt that you're stuck with."

We both erupted into laughter.

This ongoing joke, first shared as teenagers, never failed to amuse us. Most of the humor stemmed from the irony of our conversation. Heidi was athletic, model-thin at nearly 6 feet tall, with long blonde hair, appealingly freckled skin, and a beautiful face. That is what made our inside joke so funny – more irony than truth.

I went to the dining room and gave Heidi a hug and kiss. "I love the card," I told her. "See you in the morning around nine-thirty. Happy Easter. Love ya, Midget."

She squeezed me tight and planted a kiss on my cheek. "Ditto."

I watched as she walked through the dining room door and out to the kitchen. "Happy Easter. Love you Mom and Dad," she called over her shoulder.

Then I heard the kitchen door close behind her.

We heard the car pull out of the driveway. Brett tapped the horn in a "Good-bye" beep.

~ 40 ~

Candy wrappers began to litter the end tables as we dove into the high-calorie snacks. Soda cans were popped open. The movie began.

Heidi enjoyed spending time with Brett and his family. Although I wished she stayed with us, I am glad his family had time with her on Saturday too.

Ed and I enjoyed the time spent with my parents to watch a movie before returning home.

Life did not get much better.

As night descended on New Haven, I snuggled into bed. Anticipation for holiday festivities to come in the morning made it hard to sleep. Due to work schedules and varying dinner times and locations, I would not be celebrating Easter with my family on Sunday. Ed would take me to work and then join his family for church and dinner. Brett would meet Heidi at her place of employment and then join his family, knowing Heidi's arrival was only a matter of time. My parents would sleep in and enjoy the day together remembering our pre-Easter celebration Saturday evening.

I closed my eyes, reflecting on the time spent together.

Easter goodies, a movie, and laughter shared together transitioned to our last family memory with Heidi.

The car horn beeped to say, "See you later."

The answering machine beeped, "Heidi is missing."

The first beep sounded with joy and anticipation. The next, with fear, and dread.

Our priceless moments transition into precious memories before our very eyes.

Later never came…

CHAPTER 4

...and a time to laugh
Ecclesiastes 3:4a

I have not seen my sister since that Saturday evening in April at my parents' home. Agendas changed. My plan to visit Heidi at her work, example.

Return to Easter Sunday

Instead of Heidi's, "Happy Easter, Sis," with coffee and conversation...mystery and grief greeted me at the road. If only.

To wait. To stand.

Cheeks moistened with tears.

Moved to the New Haven Fire Hall without realizing it.

Now...I sat ...and waited.

Fear, anger, and loss welled up inside me. These are emotions with the power to drag one down to despair if the focus. Outside of finding my sister, I became one of these people. Law enforcement agencies and search parties arrived with such speed and precision, and the fear of this reality pierced my heart.

What if they didn't find Heidi? I was not strong enough for this. What if someone else disappeared? Why Heidi? Who is next? Her abductors remained nameless and faceless. I felt like the room was spinning out of control. I was in the hub of this spiral with no set destination. Into the dark and unknown, grief started to move in.

Why Heidi? Why today? I thought Easter is a time of celebration and rejoicing, God. Do you see us down here? Why did YOU take my only sister? Why?

Many "why's" without answers.

With my heart threatening to beat out of my chest and my face red and blotchy, anger overcame me. I started to play the blame game, with no one safe from my wrath. Initially my thoughts blamed the store's owners and their lack of safety precautions such as cameras or bells.

Of course, the array of emotions toward my sister's abductors continued. First, anger because they used the lack of security to their advantage, leaving no recorded evidence to aide in the investigation but the bulk of my anger, landed with God, the one I believed to be responsible.

After Heidi's kidnapping, I learned firsthand the range of emotions and stressors the families of America's missing children face. Have you seen the parents on the news pleading for their child's safe return? It tugs at your heart.

You ask yourself, "How do they do it? They are so strong.", but when forced into this nightmare firsthand, you learn that the strength seen for a few minutes on the news is out of necessity and might be all they had for the entire day.

The initial kidnapping ripped my heart out and then the search process put salt in the open wound, intensifying the pain with each minute. I watched the same newscasts as the public, but this time, I was live on the scene and not in the comfort of my living room.

The search for a missing person is more than a media interview or a face on a milk carton. It requires a unified, diligent, persistent, and constant effort, especially from the family and their community. It is a team effort, where no one rests until the missing and his or her parents are reunited.

My desire to help find my sister and feel like I was part of the team created additional stress and negative thoughts. I watched hundreds of people arrive to aid in the search. I was only good enough to watch. In spite of the magnitude of the search, no one found Heidi.

I asked to join the search teams but the answer was always the same: "No." This answer only intensified the anger and hurt directly related to

Heidi's kidnapping. All I wanted to do was find my sister, so why couldn't I be an active part of the process?

Why couldn't I help search? Was I only good enough to sit in a corner? I could do something. Didn't anyone know or care that I was here? In spite of the festival of people surrounding me, I felt unimportant. Each time these thoughts started to overtake my mind, God sent a volunteer on His behalf.

My gut told me to stand up, scream, and throw a fit. I started to comply when kind and caring voices interrupted my thoughts, "Lisa, I brought you a drink." or, "Can I get you something to eat?" or, "Your grandmother just sent warm cookies. Lisa...Lisa?" Their voices snapped me back to reality.

Generosity and compassion accompanied the reassurance of words. These acts of kindness saved me embarrassment. I said, "Thank you," instead of the screams I longed to release. Life saving moments disguised, as a volunteer, bringing refreshment.

Hope and love delivered via nourishment. The frustration of "not doing" remained, but food seemed to dull the pain. In less than a month, I gained thirty pounds and lost all hope.

Reflection

As I look back at photos and news clippings from those first hours, I am amazed at the composure I reflected because it was not how I felt on the inside. Of course, people would understand if I fell apart. Although it would be acceptable, something inside kept telling me to keep smiling. I felt as if I was functioning in a daze with only my thoughts to occupy me.

The notion of my words hurting someone's feelings, or worse, intensifying their grief, helped to keep my tongue in control. Sometimes though, I had a lot to say but was not able to articulate those thoughts.

Feelings Suppressed

As children, Heidi and I shared a record player. If we danced, or jumped too hard, the album would scratch. The next time we played our favorite album, the needle would sink into the divot and play that part of the song repeatedly. Our favorite part was ruined by the scratch and unable to move forward to continue the song. Regardless of how much we love some things and some people, scratches happen. We need to learn to live with the scar, it is evidence of things in our life that have made us who we are today.

Heidi's kidnapping had the same effect on my life. I was unable to move forward and unable to move beyond the hurt burrowed deep in my heart. My only sister was missing and I didn't know how to fix it, or if I could. My mind played the same questions repeatedly. *Why Heidi? Where is she? Is she still alive? Will we ever find her? Can I survive this?*

Evening, morning, and noon
I cry out in distress,
And he hears my voice.
Psalm 55:17

CHAPTER 5

A time to mourn...
Ecclesiastes 3:4b

Words have such power, to lift up or tear down. The reiteration of my own thoughts, compounded with those on the news, was the fertilizer for internal destruction. I did not share my rants, questions, or concerns with others because I feared they would think ill of me.

Not even my husband truly knew. On the rare occasion when Ed could get me to leave the *Heidi Allen Search Center*, he attempted to draw out the emotions bottled within me.

"Lisa, you need to talk to me. I can't help if you do not share. Neither of us can live like this."

"I don't know what you want me to say, Ed. Everyone thinks Heidi is dead. But what if..." and the tears flooded his shoulder.

"I don't care who you talk to, just talk to someone. Maybe your parents?"

NO. I would not be one more worry or burden in their lives. They had enough to deal with. Mom and Dad focused their attention where it needed to be, to find Heidi.

I honestly believed no one would want to listen to me. Worse yet, if they did, they would know how selfish and uncaring I was. I was not sure how to express myself without the guilt associated with it. I knew deep down Ed would listen without judgment. I also knew my parents would want me to share with them. I set reasoning aside and lived in the moment.

I could not work. I held myself captive within the confines of the search center. I slept in folding chairs and on military cots at the search center because I was too afraid something would break in the case and I wouldn't be there. I only went home when forced.

Family and friends attempted to encourage me but their body language spoke a different language than the sound exiting their mouths.

One volunteer said, "Everything will be okay. There are a lot of people looking for her," and return to his or her assignment as one hand wiped the tears welling in their eyes.

Another might say, "People are distributing flyers all over, even on the thruway. We're going to find Heidi," as they fought back tears.

My Gram was a notorious "people watcher". To avoid some of the inner voices shouting at me I started to carry on this family trait. I chose to ignore the words spoken and focused on what they weren't saying and the heavy sighs before they spoke.

Exhales with enough force to blow out the birthday candles on one's cake combined with moisture-filled eyes that eventually began to leak, "I'm sorry. I don't know why I am crying. I'm so sorrrr..." The voice trailed off as they walked away but the trembling in their body remained in plain sight.

First, it was consolation, then sympathy. "I don't know how you are doing this." or, "You will probably never see your sister again. You are so strong. I would be a basket case." And the most common was, "I wish I could do more."

Go away. If I could fall to the floor in the fetal position and cry my eyes out, I would. But how would that help my parents?

I was NOT strong but I recognized the need to be something I was not. The last thing I wanted to do was wear a princess crown of pity and draw attention away from the search. I kept these thoughts secret until the publication of this book.

"You could do it, if you had to," was always my response. I learned firsthand we might not think we can do something until we are face-to-face with it.

"I don't think so, Lisa. I can barely make coffee but you're offering to help everywhere, making phone calls, and visiting with everyone you can." More tears...she walked away.

Flashback to a conversation with Heidi

A few years prior to Heidi's kidnapping, Heidi and I followed the search for twelve-year-old Sara Anne Wood with disbelief.

"Lisa, what if they never find her?"

"I don't know, but it is terrible. The only thing I do know is I couldn't do it. What would I do without you, Heidi? You are more than a sister, you are my friend."

"You don't have to worry. We live in New Haven, New York. We don't even have a stoplight."

"Thank goodness." I didn't think I could do it then with Heidi standing next to me. *How would I ever survive this?* All I had was guilt. Instead of worrying about the torture Heidi must have been enduring, if she was alive, I wasted time reflecting on my own weakness. I needed to focus, if not for my own benefit then for my parents.

The Reality

To most, I appeared to be functioning and of great help. Each minute Heidi was missing my heart slowly followed, losing strength and faith. My love and respect for my parents, combined with the overwhelming appreciation for all the community was doing, kept me moving.

If complete strangers could set aside their lives to help then the least I could do was force myself to do the same.

Everyone worked tirelessly to find Heidi. Sheriff Nellis reminded the search teams and my family daily: "Heidi Allen is missing. This is a forcible abduction. Each minute Heidi is missing, the less likely she is to return."

As if I needed a reminder, not. At least he cared enough to make sure others understood. Minutes turned to hours and hope turned to despair.

I lost more than a sister on that bitter Easter morning. I lost a friend, and began to lose my faith in humanity, and most importantly in God. Death is not new. I have lost loved ones to cancer, diabetes, and old age.

None of these prepare one for the tragedy associated with the abduction and "missing" status you live with after the initial trauma. The biggest difference is time.

The time spent holding a loved one's hand in their last days is a precious gift. It is an opportunity to express your love, learn some family secrets, and listen. This time opens the door to say good-bye and slowly let go, whereas tragedy is unexpected, with no "Good-bye".

I didn't know how to handle this sudden loss. Most told me, "Pray. God will answer your prayers." or, "Lisa, God can take away your pain but you need to ask first." *Whatever, why should I pray to a God who let Heidi disappear?* No one can take away this pain.

Even though I walk through the valley
Of the shadow of death,
I will fear no evil,
For you are with me;
Your rod and your staff,
They comfort me.
Psalm 23:4

CHAPTER 6

And a time to dance...
Ecclesiastes 3:4b

It is difficult to trust the unknown, especially with the media reporting such catastrophes and tragedy on a daily basis, if not with each new broadcast. Prior to Heidi's kidnapping, Sara Anne Wood's disappearance was the only one I knew of in our state of New York. Of course, this was my naiveté, not fact. Kidnapping is not isolated to our small town or even our state.

Kidnapping is not new

Known as "The Crime of the Century", the oldest case I heard of occurred in 1932. The twenty-month-old son of aviator Charles Lindbergh was kidnapped from his New Jersey home. I read about this case as a teenager and remember watching a movie too. My heart ached for this little boy and his family. At least it was just a movie, or so I thought.

I was unable to fathom how the family could deal with this unspeakable tragedy. The Lindbergh baby had five siblings that would grow up without their brother. I could never live without my sister. As I read the credits, "Based on a true story", I cried and ran to my mom for assurance.

"Why would someone do that to an innocent baby?" No words spoken, Mom simply held me, brushed the hair from my eyes, and hummed. Her love comforted me.

Kidnapping is more common than most people think. It happens to ordinary people, like six-year-old Adam Walsh in 1981, Sara Anne Wood in 1993, and my sister in 1994.

Adam Walsh was kidnapped from a department store in Florida and his case was made into a movie within a couple years.

Yes, I watched this one too. I found the mystery fascinating and terrifying at the same time. I didn't want to watch another minute butI hoped and waited for the successful conclusion. No one would make a movie if there weren't a successful conclusion, right?

"Mom, he is only a year younger than Heidi. What would you do if it were Heidi or me?"

"It isn't, so I will not even think about it and neither should you."

"But, Mom."

"Lisa, if you can't watch these movies without stressing yourself out, I won't let you watch them anymore. Do you understand?"

"Yes."

"Good. Now go outside and play with your sister."

"Mom, look." The television screen stole my attention from my mother

Adam Walsh's father, John Walsh, spoke at the end of the movie. He shared his heart with America on behalf of his son with his mission to help keep other children safe. *Wow. First, he loses his son and now he is working to help others.*

John Walsh started the television show *America's Most Wanted,* and helped to form the *National Center for Missing and Exploited Children* (NCMEC). The Walsh family is a living witness of God's strength and love in the way they have channeled their grief to prevent other parents from experiencing a similar situation and to help others find their missing child.

My parents and sister are among this list. Within days of Heidi's kidnapping, camera crews arrived. Interviews, filming, and observation developed into Heidi's case being one of the featured "most wanted" on April 9. I never thought anyone I knew would be on this show, much less my only sister. It was both an honor and devastating blow to have *America's Most Wanted* feature my sister's case. All I could do was cry.

Reality sets in

First Sara, now Heidi... Nearly eight months and one-hundred miles separated the two upstate New York tragedies. Months prior to Heidi's kidnapping, while Heidi and I searched for the perfect dress and jewelry for my upcoming wedding, the Wood family searched for their sweet and precious daughter, Sara.

Woven into our discussions of who would decorate the reception hall on Saturday morning while we were at the hairdressers were conversations of the recent developments in Sara's case. Although we never met Sara, Heidi was so upset.

"Lisa, she is just a little girl. Why does someone do that? What if they drove through here? What can we do?"

"I don't know. Pray?" Ironic isn't it, this is the first thing I suggested for another missing child but when it was my own sister, Heidi, it was the last thing I wanted to hear.

It is overwhelming to me when I think that Heidi and I talked about a little girl we didn't know only to have Heidi on the missing person flyer hanging alongside Sara's months into the future. We spoke about the unlikelihood of an abduction occurring so close to us. Only God knew what would happen the following April. Heidi too, became one of the missing.

In 1994, I could only name a few missing children, but today I not only can name them, I know some of their families personally thanks to the Ride for Missing Children, an outreach triggered through Mr. Wood's determination and Mr. Walsh's center.

Abduction and kidnapping happen on a daily basis. Children, teens, and adults are taken against their will. Most are never seen again. Photographs of innocence with "MISSING" stamped above or below it tear at the heart. Their pictures, most with smiling faces, hang on bulletin boards in stores and law enforcement agencies. Their families live each day wondering, *Will they find my loved one today?*

Each Case Is Different

Not all missing person cases make national news like the Lindbergh or Walsh kidnappings. Not all parents have the capacity or strength to do more than survive. Not all parents can advocate for other people's children by keeping them safer through their missions.

Each case is no less important. Heidi is my sister. Her disappearance devastated our family. I am not spearheading a local or national organization. And I am not making a movie-of-the-week. I am writing to share how this tragedy influenced and changed my life.

It is an illustration of how God worked for good in an instance where there didn't seem to be any. It took me a decade after Heidi's kidnapping to understand this. I pray this book will save you from similar lost years in search of something or someone to fill the void left because of your sibling's absence.

You might be reading this book because you hope to fill the emptiness left in your heart. On the other hand, you may have found true Joy and the answer to this search. Either way, I welcome you and thank you for setting aside time to see how God healed the hurt and worked for good in a tough situation.

Praise be to the God and Father
Of our Lord Jesus Christ,
The Father of compassion
And the God of all comfort…
2 Corinthians 1:3

CHAPTER 7

A time to scatter stones ...
Ecclesiastes 3:5a

The Lindbergh family relied on the daily newspaper and the telephone to distribute their son's photograph and information to the public. New technologies offer quicker distribution and vital minutes are used instead of lost. We had more avenues available to get word out to the public. In comparison to today's capabilities though, it was still miniscule. Even though there have been a multitude of changes and advances in technology, abducted children remain missing.

Media in 1994

As with any missing person's case, media coverage is essential. In 1994, we didn't have the luxury of sending a text or email from our cellular phones to friends, family and our social networking groups. We first contacted the media via fax machines, telephones and cellular phones. Internet usage and availability were just starting to make an impression on the world so this was not a primary way to reach the public.

Cellular phones and computers existed in the early nineties but not in the same capacity. The cellular phone resided in a bag, not in your back pocket, and resembled a portable version of your house phone. The computers were monstrous and their connection speed was as slow as the computer was big.

If you were one of the few to have a home computer, it was too big to sit on your lap while watching television. Our computers required an entire desk's top with a slide-drawer for the keyboard because it didn't fit on the desk. As if the size of the desk was not a design challenge in itself, it also needed to be located near a phone outlet.

I know it is hard to believe, but Wi-Fi was not an option in 1994. If you had a computer with Internet access then you used something called "dial-up". The only way to connect to the Internet was through the telephone line. If you needed the Internet and a phone call to make, a decision was necessary of which to do first.

You didn't have the option to text one friend, IM another, update your status and talk to grandma on the landline all at the same time. You could call someone *or* use the Internet, but never both at the same time.

We relied heavily on local television and newspapers to disseminate Heidi's information to the public. While the media can be extremely helpful, they were competing with the other media on site for the "best" story so there were officers designated to arrange the press conferences and interviews with the family.

Why do I tell you this? Good question. Although cellular phones, personal computers, and the Internet were on the upswing, not everyone wanted or could afford these high-tech items. We needed to get the word out about Heidi's disappearance as quickly as possible. Choices were necessary. Did we call or email our friends and family? Who was willing to leave to do this? Would it even help?

We had to think and prioritize how we accessed our technology in a quick and efficient manner because each minute wasted was a minute further away from finding Heidi. It was life-and-death.

In addition to the radio communications of law enforcement to other agencies, each other, and the media, we set in motion to do everything we knew how to do.

We started only with Dad's cellular phone hooked up to a converter box on the wall to contact family, friends and the media. The first missing person's flier made for Heidi was on a home PC and printer. Nothing fancy, but simple like Heidi. It served the purpose. The flyer contained the necessary information of her photograph, height, weight, skin, eye and hair colors and a number to contact with any information. As soon as the flyer was printed and brought to the center, faxing, copying, and distribution began.

My father's boss left his family for the day to help with the distribution of Heidi's missing person's flyer. He made the fifteen-minute drive from Oswego in order to expand the exposure of Heidi's picture and her disappearance across the country and beyond. He promptly returned to Oswego and faxed it to Lafarge's twenty-three terminals on the Great Lakes and in Canada.

Our family joined the community to fax media on the donated fax machines and started printing our makeshift flyer on the donated copy machines. Others sent flyers of Heidi across the country and Canada.

Ed and I used Dad's cell phone to call anyone and everyone we could think of. Those first two months, my parents' cell phone bills were over $3,000. In comparison, this was a small price to pay if even one of those phone calls brought their youngest daughter, my sister, home again.

The media arrived within minutes to cover the case. We had newspapers, radio and television stations sharing Heidi's photograph and pertinent information. I was impressed with the amount of coverage and support provided to both law enforcement and our family. In spite of this, it was not enough.

Our limited technology and access to media did have one benefit though: control. Press conferences and interviews were the only way the media obtained any information. Their presence on the scene was mandatory if they wanted the most current story. This is a task much harder to accomplish in today's techno-world.

I wait for the LORD,

My soul waits,

And in his word I put my hope.

My soul waits for the Lord

More than watchmen wait for the morning,

More than watchmen wait for the morning.

Psalm 130:5-6

CHAPTER 8

...and a time to gather them.
Ecclesiastes 3:5a

Every second is vital when someone is abducted, and those seconds added together equal the most crucial minutes in the quest to find the missing. Heidi's last transaction, two packs of generic cigarettes, printed at 7:42 a.m. The first officer arrived around 7:45 a.m. In less than three minutes, my sister vanished.

Customers entered the store after this last transaction, and before law enforcement arrived. With their own schedules to keep and no apparent alarm over the missing clerk, they tossed their money on the counter and left. The kidnappers manipulated the town's trust and innocence to fulfill their plan: to abduct Heidi Allen.

A Command Center Is Birthed

My memories transitioned from being alone at the *D & W Convenience store* one moment to sitting in a corner at the New Haven Volunteer Fire Corporation (NHVFC) the next. With the D & W an official crime scene, the NHVFC graciously offered their building as a base for the investigation. The banquet hall commonly used for weddings and celebrations transformed into the "Heidi Allen Command Center" within minutes.

Instead of balloons and bouquets of flowers, the room now resembled the interior of the Sheriff's Department, complete with uniformed officers, desks overflowing with papers, fax machines, telephones, and copiers printing flyers by the hundreds. Conversations and theories pertaining to Heidi's disappearance melded together.

Grief's Power on the Mind

To this day, I am not even sure how I came to be at the fire hall. I needed help from the experts, my husband and parents. I prayed their memories were better than mine was.

"Ed, do you know how I came to be at the fire hall and how my car made it to the parking lot?" The discussion that followed added more mystery and confusion.

My husband, Ed said he didn't know who gave me a ride but he assured me I did *not* drive. "You weren't yourself and looked out of it so I kept the keys when I left with your uncle," he said.

I didn't even have my own car keys. This was not getting clearer but I knew whom to ask next.

We drove to my parents' house so I could ask this same question with hopes of a different response. *Boy was I wrong.*

"Hey Kid. What's up? You have that look on your face." Concern flooded Dad's face.

"I'm sorry to bother you with this, but I need to know. Do you remember how I made it from the store to the fire hall?"

Dad was first to respond. "You rode with Mom."

"Ken, Lisa didn't ride with me. She rode with Kris." A pause, "Or did she ride with me?" Mom's indecisive tone told me this was going to be an interesting conversation.

"Ed went with Unc and took my keys with him so I had to ride with someone, but I have no recollection who."

"As soon as the deputies finished interviewing your mother and me, I jumped in my truck to help with the search."

"Mom, did you drive yourself?"

"I don't know now. Maybe we both rode with someone else. Ed, did you give Lisa's keys to someone?"

"I don't know, Sue. I don't remember. Sorry."

"Nothing to be sorry about, Ed. Is it that important to the story, Lisa?"

"I guess not. I want the most accurate recollection of our first day. Do I tell people I am clueless and lost days, months, and years of my life?"

"I think you have your answer. Stick to your guns, be honest, and people will understand." With a wink and a smile, Dad returned to the living room. *He knows me so well, one of many things I love about him.*

"The only thing we know is that you didn't drive yourself because Ed had your keys." Mom continued, "Thanks to your curiosity I don't even know how I got there." Laughter erupted. We spent more than an hour talking about how much we didn't remember.

The entire conversation concluded with an important realization: tragedy influences the memory more than we realize at the time.

Back to the Heidi Allen Search Center, 1994

The next thing I remember was someone directing me to a chair. Although I assured them I was okay and would prefer to help, I was told, "Please sit down, honey, and we'll take care of everything."

With nothing to do but think, I withdrew into myself and tried to sort through the thoughts flooding my head.

I remembered seeing Heidi at my parents' house the night before. I remembered the laughter and notion of seeing her again in the morning.

I remembered standing at the gasoline pump and watching the sheriff's department tape off the "crime scene", establish a roadblock and interview family, co-workers, and anyone driving by. All these memories became an escape as I re-created them in my mind since there was nothing else I could do.

I observed many interactions between law enforcement and the drivers stopped at the roadblock in the intersection in front of the *D & W Convenience Store*. I couldn't hear their conversation or even read their lips, but I watched their facial expressions and body language.

To keep myself from crying or screaming, I tried to imagine what they were saying to each other.

Illustration by Mary M. Buske, 2012

~ 71 ~

Mentally transported back to the intersection, I manifest how one conversation might have sounded.

Officer: Good morning, we are conducting an investigation. Did you drive through this intersection this morning?

Driver: I'm on my way to church. What happened?

Officer: A young woman was abducted while working alone this morning. So, is this your first time through here this morning?

Driver: No sir. I...I...Oh no. Not here. Not in New Haven. (Wiping tears from her face) Tell the family we will be praying. This is terrible, just terrible.

Officer: Thank you and if you do hear of someone that may have traveled this route between 7:30 a.m. and 8:00 a.m., please have them contact the Oswego County Sheriff or stop at the command center being set up at the NHVC.

The sheriff's department was diligent and stopped each car. People were understanding of the delay once they learned why they were stopped. *How many of these people would share this information with their clergy and family when they arrived to their destination? Would this help find Heidi?*

Mom tapped me on my shoulder, "Lisa, are you okay? What are you thinking about?"

"Nothing important. Do you need me?"

"No, just need to know you are all right."

"I'm okay Mom, don't worry about me."

Of course, on the inside I was falling apart. This was the last thing I would share with my parents. They didn't need one more thing to worry about. They were suffering a parent's worst fear: their child was missing.

Do nothing out of selfish ambition or vain conceit,

But in humility consider others above yourselves.

Each of you should look not only to your own interests,

But also to the interests of others.

Philippians 2:3-4

CHAPTER 9
...a time to embrace...
Ecclesiastes 3:5b

We were equipped to handle and respond to more than we could ever have imagined. Heidi's disappearance was evidence of this. Although no trained missing person's expert lived in this upstate New York town, protocol and structure organized quickly with determination and heart.

Banquet Hall to Command & Search Center

Sheriff Nellis and his team took a proactive approach to establish the necessary boundaries and guidelines. Before noon, the large banquet hall transitioned into seven distinctive areas. Each section had a specific purpose vital to the investigation. Donated wall dividers helped to section off the room. Signs identified each particular area with the necessary furniture and equipment added. The room of celebration was gone, just like Heidi.

The seven areas established were:

- Family
- Law Enforcement
- Search and Rescue
- Kitchen/Food
- Media, search

- Copying
- General meeting area in the center

There were three entrances to the "Command Center" portion of the fire department. One's affiliation and purpose for being there determined which entrance to use. The doors had hand-written signs on the outside to avoid confusion.

"Mom, why are we using this door? I never even knew it was here."

"The investigators said it would be better if we, Heidi's immediate family, used the same entrance as them to avoid a lot of questions from the media. It also makes it easier to come and go when you are tired of pretending to smile."

"Oh, can I still use the other door?"

"Of course. This is an option, not a mandate."

The volunteers, news media and the rest of our family entered through the West entrance, perpendicular to the East entrance, designated for law enforcement.

By day's end, only law enforcement and my parents used this entrance. The volunteer fire department personnel used the North side entrance off the bay. The fire engines, dispatch, and fire chief's office remained in the bay along with the men and women's restrooms. The kitchen was located on the south side of the building. No entry was allowed from the kitchen, again for security purposes.

With security measures in place, countless volunteers started to arrive. Crossing the threshold, they went to work. Not one asked a question, but only joined in the efforts to find Heidi.

How would we ever let them know how thankful we are? Was it even possible?

Meanwhile, I stood, sat and paced in the family corner, dazed, confused, and lost. I didn't know how to help or what I could do to lend a hand.

Every time I asked, "Can I help you with that?" the answer was the same. "Oh, let me do that for you. You have done so much already. Have a seat and relax." Rather than cause a scene, I returned to my corner to sit and wait. Everyone thought the family corner was a place of relaxation but in truth, it was a sentence.

I wondered if they were really saying something like, "Poor girl has lost her sister. She does not need to work too." In hindsight, I understand people wanted to give me time to grieve and deal with what happened. With each refusal, my sense of helplessness and isolation deepened.

My parents were in and out of the "family" section all the time. They would check on me, rest for a moment and then they were off to "do" whatever needed to be done. Other family members also utilized our section as a refuge but no one ever stayed long.

There were always people coming through the doors but at the same time, I was lonely. I could not put my finger on it then, but as I reread the news articles and my notes for this book, I realized why I was so lonely.

Plain and simple, I lost my sister, and my friend. While others were using their gifts and skills to assist with the search, I was just there, longing for someone to fill the void.

I longed to fill the emptiness but I wasn't allowed to do anything. Volunteers, law enforcement, and family reiterated similar thoughts. "Where is Heidi? We have to find her, soon." Family and friends worked to answer this pressing question. I did not.

Did I really want to help or was I truly content to watch everyone else? Have I even eaten today? How could I do anything that requires logical thinking?

I am not one to sit still for any length of time, especially when under stress. Letting my mind wander allowed me to leave the chair mentally while my physical self remained stagnant.

I don't remember too many people actually talking to me. They were busy assisting with the search in one manner or another. I was thankful for the outpouring of support.

The righteous cry out, and the LORD hears them;

He delivers them from all their troubles.

The LORD is close to the brokenhearted

And saves those who are crushed in spirit.

The righteous person may have many troubles,

But the LORD delivers him from them all;

Psalm 34:17 – 19

CHAPTER 10

And a time to refrain...
Ecclesiastes 3:5b

Although this was the first abduction in our town, if not in all of Oswego County, you would not have known it by watching everyone work together to establish a home base and unified search. The Oswego County Sheriff's Department led the investigation with support from outside agencies, including the FBI.

Community members arrived throughout the day to assist with the search efforts. Family, friends and those we had yet to meet ventured from their traditional Easter rituals in order to be together at the Command Center. Everyone's goal was the same, to bring Heidi home.

The Oswego County Sheriff's Department was the first on the scene and the lead investigating unit. They set aside agency prides as they teamed up with the FBI, local politicians, the armed forces, and a missing person's specialist to investigate New Haven's first kidnapping.

They exercised professionalism and heart in all their efforts. I wonder if all missing persons' families have this type of team effort. *Do the pieces all fall into place as quickly and easily as they did for us? Would I meet anyone else who has lost a loved one?*

Inside the command center, the sheriff's deputies and investigators were hard at work. From my vantage point in the family section, I could easily observe every aspect of the investigation and the people involved.

A Shocking Statement

I asked one of the sheriff's deputies, "Why are you so concerned with watching the doors?" I could not imagine why watching volunteers enter and exit was important.

The answer was both overwhelming and upsetting. "Most criminals return to the scene of the crime. It gives them a thrill," was the deputy's reply.

His response made me nauseous. I shook my head in disbelief as someone helped me to the nearest chair. "Why?" was the only word I uttered. The kidnapper instilled fear within our family and community. *Opened doors, now locked.* This new bit of information heightened my guard even more. I scanned the crowded room.

Among the generous, compassionate and concerned citizens, could there be the individual, or individuals, responsible for this terrible and heartbreaking journey? The majority came to serve and aid in the recovery of a missing girl. *Would Heidi's abductors returned to the scene of the crime?*

The officer spoke words of encouragement and assurance. "You are safe. Your family is safe. You have nothing to worry about." Words meant to console had an opposite effect.

He spoke words of security but I heard empty promises. If we were truly safe, we would not be looking for Heidi. I would be at work, my parents at home, and Heidi would be with Brett's family. My brain could not comprehend one more detail so I accepted his words at face value.

The Investigation Intensifies

The officers and investigators worked diligently and I marveled at the organized chaos surrounding me. Officers, stationed around the southeast corner, were conducting interviews, fielding phone calls and following up on incoming tips. People delivering updated information constantly surrounded the lead investigators.

Along with the uniformed officers, I remember hearing a rumor about undercover officers working as "volunteers". Initially, I viewed this good investigating as deceptive to the community. This allowed the Sheriff's Department to gain an insider's view of the case. The undercover officers were able to listen to details possibly overlooked and not shared with a uniformed officer. It allowed for a different form of communication and investigation while also protecting the family from further harm.

The community initially organized the search and rescue efforts with guidance from the sheriff's department. Law enforcement and volunteers worked together to monitor and track the search missions. Maps of all types covered every available wall and table space. I never knew there were so many different types of maps available.

In a coordinated effort, one examined the road map and another viewed the physical map. Across the table, another studied the topographical map. Three different views of the same area, allowed for a more defined and specific search.

The calm composure of the volunteers as they received their "assignments" amazed me. I wanted to help find my sister but the answer was always the same. "No, please have a seat, Lisa."

I didn't want to sit anymore. I didn't want to pace in the corner for another second. I wanted to help. It was not my lack of skill holding me back but instead my relation to the case. Heidi was my sister so searching was not an option.

Other members of my family continued to help, unaware I was waiting for an opportunity to join them. The only ones requested to stay on the sidelines were the parents and siblings, for reasons I didn't understand at the time. While I didn't like to sit and watch, this taught me to have an open heart and mind to accept help from others.

Regardless of the assignment, everyone worked with determination and heart. I remember thinking, *The entire sheriff's department must be here. Who is home with their families?* Then it dawned on me: we were not the only ones affected by Heidi's abduction.

Selflessness Exemplified

As I looked around the room and saw the families spending their Easter helping us, I cried. No one sat idle. Everyone had a task to complete with one unified goal, to find Heidi. It was at this moment I realized the importance of letting everyone do his or her job. They wanted to find Heidi as much as I wanted her found. This was no time for my pride to step in. Everyone wanted to help and care for me. I only needed to let them. Why was this so hard?

I don't remember the exact time during that first day when this realization hit, but I remember crying until there were no more tears to cry. Why? I wanted my sister back. Who held me while I cried? I don't know but someone enveloped me in a hug.

Help is necessary and it opens the door for God's blessings and provision, especially when in your greatest need. If we recognize this, it makes it easier to accept it.

The Lord is my strength and my shield.
My heart trusts in him,
And I am helped. My heart leaps for joy
And I will give thanks to him in song.
Psalm 28:7

How do I trust after something like this? Will I ever learn to trust again? Will I accept help more willingly? Only God could work this miracle in my heart.

"You're going to be okay. We are going to find her. It is okay. Let it out." The words repeated softly in my ear as they rocked me gently in their arms like a mother comforting her baby, so much love. *Why did sadness still consume me?*

The LORD is close to the brokenhearted
And saves those who are crushed in spirit.
Psalm 34:18

CHAPTER 11
A time to plant...
Ecclesiastes 3:2b

"What If?" Questions

Were the customers who left their money on the counter plagued by the "What if"? *What if I woke up ten minutes earlier? What if I looked around? What if I contacted the store manager? Called the sheriff's department? Might Heidi still be alive and safe? What if? What if we didn't ask those questions of ourselves?*

Life comes to a grinding halt when we spend our days second-guessing our decisions. To live in the present we need to focus on what happened and move forward from there. My Gram always said, "Live for the living. Life is too short."

God knew which customer would take the time to look and which one would continue on their way. God orchestrated the deputy's drive that morning. God used a familiar face to catch the attention of the officer, assuring he would stop.

In those first years, I focused on, "If the deputy had only come a few minutes earlier, then Heidi would not have disappeared." Years later, I understand His timing is perfect, not a minute earlier or a minute later. The deputy's typical drive to work transitioned into one of the biggest cases he has probably worked on.

Instead of a quiet drive, he saw a man running toward the road, rapidly waving his arms. He stopped. His first case of the day brought a rude awakening to our sleepy town.

Looking Into My Parents' Eyes

The command center was evidence of the new and tragic event that took place. As people shifted around the room, I caught glimpses of my parents. The hardest part of looking into my parents' eyes was seeing their hurt and grief. Their faces were missing something.

My mother's face exhibited a heightened level of grief, greater than when my grandfather passed away when I was in third grade. The blank stare coming from the depths of my father's eyes will haunt me for years. My father didn't let life beat him down so this was the first time I witnessed defeat and pure grief on his face. While my parents were busy, everything seemed to move in slow motion around them.

I may have been sitting by myself, but through the generosity, love, and support of our community -- I had many opportunities to reflect and remember.

I remembered seeing Heidi the night before which transitioned quickly to the conversation with the officer earlier that morning. He took my photographs of Heidi and told me "...nothing is too small. Can you remember anything she said in the past few days that might help? Do you know of anyone that would want to harm your sister? Lisa, if you remember anything let us know."

I did not have answers to his questions. His words replayed in my head repeatedly until I simply could not think, or sit, anymore. I wanted to scream, *If I knew anything that would help find my sister don't you think I would have blurted it at you while running from my car? You imbecile.* Thank goodness, God controlled my tongue and kept it contained.

I walked around the room, wrestling with the continuous questions and frustrations rambling in my head. The *Heidi Allen Command Center* was coming to fruition, without any help from me.

New questions infiltrated my brain. *Who is here? How did everyone find out? Why are they here, on Easter? Will I ever know who and why? How will I ever be able to thank everyone?*

During those first days, I'm not sure when volunteers were required to sign in, but at some point it became necessary. Initially, it was to maintain control and monitor who was assisting, since "one of the volunteers could be my sister's abductor". It is still a difficult concept to wrap my mind around, but little did I know that in the months to come, this would be true in Heidi's case too.

One of the men arrested and charged for her kidnapping walked where I walked. He assisted alongside the bounty of caring citizens that were devoting their time to find Heidi. If I had known how much truth the officer spoke, I probably would have yelled instead of keeping quiet.

The Community Rallies

I felt as if I was walking in a fog until the aroma of ham, potatoes and apple pie snapped me out of it. Families, with their Easter dinners wrapped in foil, arrived as soon as they learned of Heidi's disappearance.

My parents, Ed and I would not enjoy a traditional ham at my Gram's but we would have an Easter dinner in a way never experienced before. It seemed as if every person crossing the threshold brought his or her Easter provisions to share. We lacked for nothing, our needs were met and then some.

Yet he gave a command to the skies above
And opened the doors of the heavens;
He rained down manna for the people to eat,
He gave them the grain of heaven.
Human beings ate the bread of angels;
He sent them all the food they could eat.
Psalm 78:23 – 25

While we tried to grasp the reality of Heidi's abduction, our beloved New Haven community rallied. It started with holiday dinners with broader assortments that followed in the remainder of the month. Hot meals, beverages and baked goods were blessings to our family and the thousands aiding in the search. The variety of food had the potential to make the finest bakeries envious.

Although the foods were delicious, there were other reasons to cross the threshold, the primary one, to find Heidi. As a volunteer, tables running parallel on either side of the door greeted you. The tables served primarily as dividers with the family section to the right and the copying station to the left. The tables made it easier for volunteers to track who came in and out along with their purpose for being at the center.

Official greeters staffed the tables, taking their direction from the Sheriff's department. They dedicated their time and heart daily to ensure everyone felt welcome while also maintaining a secure environment. We were overwhelmed with the support, and needed direction and help to continue.

Every person that walked through the door started with, "Have you heard anything? How can I help?" A volunteer's willingness to do whatever was necessary inspired me. I sat in awe of their strength and willingness. *I had to do something too, but what?*

You hear, O LORD, the desire of the afflicted.
You encourage them, and you listen to their cry...
Psalm 10:17

CHAPTER 12

And a time to uproot...
Ecclesiastes 3:2b

The first month of Heidi's disappearance rendered me unable to function. I took multiple leave of absences from the Sunrise Nursing Home. The first leave was directly after Heidi's disappearance with more following so I could join my family in the courtroom to hear the cases against the men charged with Heidi's kidnapping and presumed death. My inability to think or focus prevented quality and safety in a work environment.

I wasn't the only one rendered incapable to function in the real world. My parents, aunts, and uncles found themselves on temporary leaves of absence too. Heidi's disappearance crippled their mental and physical health, making it impossible to work ever again.

Even Ed took a brief leave himself so he could help in the search and be there for me when I needed him. We only left the search center when we absolutely needed to, which was not often.

I spent my nights sleeping on a cot or in a chair with my head propped against the wall at the *Heidi*

Allen Search Center. Quality sleep to promote health wasn't a priority, but my presence at the center was.

Eventually we moved from the NHVFC to my parents' house, sleeping on their pullout couch. Unable to handle the thought of not being there when news came in, we went home long enough to shower, change, and check the answering machine.

> *The churning inside me never stops;*
> *Days of suffering confront me.*
> *My harp is tuned to mourning,*
> *And my flute to the sound of wailing.*
> Job 30:27, 31

One night I overheard my parents having a discussion at the kitchen table. Dad's words tugged at my heart. "I'm worried about Lisa. What are we going to do? I will not lose another daughter."

What had I done? I thought I was holding it together. The last thing I wanted was my parents to worry about me. Should I interrupt?

"I know. She is here physically but that is it. She is lost without Heidi. It hit her hard." Mom's tears flowed as if they would never stop.

I tried to keep my emotions, fears, and thoughts to myself. My parents didn't need additional stress. *That was never my plan. I am sorry. I thought I was making it easier.*

"Ken, Heidi's friend Suzie is still organizing the news articles. Lisa always perks up when she is around. We could ask Lisa to help Suzie with the newspapers?"

"Great idea. It will be good for both of them. We'll tell her in the morning."

I cried myself to sleep in the other room as I realized I created more stress instead of eliminating it. Mixed emotions for upsetting my parents coupled with a thankful heart overcame me. At least I had something to do the next morning when I returned to the center.

Finally I Can Help

The next day, Mom shared her idea with Suzie and me. I could see why Heidi and Suzie were such good friends. Suzie introduced me to everyone and we got to work. Seeds of friendship planted in the midst of tragedy.

There were so many articles. I was overwhelmed. "Where do all the newspapers come from?"

Suzie chuckled. "Volunteers bring them or people leave them on their way to work."

"Really?"

"Yeah, your family even brings them. There are papers from Watertown, New York and even some from out-of-state. It is pretty cool to know Heidi's picture and flyer is across the country."

Her excitement created nausea. That couldn't be a good thing. Heidi was missing and ripped from our lives. *I was supposed find joy in Heidi's face plastered all over the newspaper? Not.*

Thankfully, my face only showed interest, not my inner turmoil.

Suzie continued. "Our first responsibility is to read through the paper and cut out all the articles about your sister's case. Make sure you check the editorials too."

I only read one article and it upset me so much I decided not to read another one. Do I tell Suzie? Maybe this was not a good idea.

"I don't read the articles, I just can't. I'm sorry."

Before Suzie could respond, another volunteer joined the conversation. "No worries, there are enough people here who want to read the articles. You can skip that part." *Phew.*

As if to change the subject, Suzie added, "Will you sort the cut articles by date first then by morning or evening edition? The only thing you will need to look at is the newspaper's name and the date. Sound good?"

"I didn't realize how cumbersome this job is. Thank you. I am sorry if I have not thanked you before. I'm glad you are each here."

Suzie smiled from ear-to-ear. "It isn't that bad. Look at all the coverage Heidi is getting. You never know if one of these photos or articles will be the one to bring her home." *Wow. This was why she was excited. How did she stay so positive? She is one amazing young woman.*

I accepted Suzie's outlook as my own and it lightened my mood. The monotonous task of sorting newspaper clippings became something I looked forward to each day. After sorting, we photocopied, hole-punched, and placed the copies in a binder for my parents, and me, to read in the far future.

The actual newspaper clipping, preserved on white poster board with glue. When one side was full, a protective layer of clear contact paper covered the entire side. Heidi would be amazed at the coverage her case received when found, if this day ever came. A little optimism returned as I thought this.

"Lisa, here is another article. It is a good picture of your parents. Don't you think?"

"Suzie, they look old." *My parents have aged decades in a matter of hours.* "There is such sadness in their eyes."

Would I ever get over this? Would I be able to look at a newspaper article or watch the news without tearing up?

"Oh Lisa, I think it is time for a break."

More Than a News Clipping

Our family has always been close, but after Heidi's kidnapping the bond was tighter. It was common for me to stop at my parents' and Gram's on a daily basis prior to Heidi's kidnapping. Friendly drop-ins morphed from habit to necessity over night. My parents needed to see me every day and I needed to see them.

Even though we saw each other every day I didn't realize the effect Heidi's kidnapping was having on them physically. Gray hair, slumped shoulders, and sad eyes encompassed by dark circles now greeted me.

Instead of vibrancy and hope, their grief-stricken frames resembled the newspaper of days earlier. *How did I miss this? When did they get old?*

The World does not Stop

One of our routine visits home reminded us, life goes on in spite of the tragedy in one's life. Bill collectors demanded our attention.

"Ed, what are we going to do?"

"Lisa, it will be okay. I promise."

"Stop making promises you can't keep. Nearly every message on the machine is someone wanting money. I am tired." *I'm done, don't they see it. I was not as strong as my parents were. How did they do it?*

CRASH! "No one cares!"

BANG! "I CAN'T do this anymore. I'm done."

Then I fell to my knees and tears raced down my cheeks. I tried to pick up the broken frame with the picture of Heidi and me smiling. More tears and broken glass surrounded me but I couldn't pick it up. All I could do was cry.

"Lisa, I am going back to work Monday."

With blurred vision, "What? Why?"

"Lisa, you are right about some things. We can't keep living with your parents. We need to pay our bills. I am going back to work. I need to, for us."

"Okay. I don't know if I can do it."

"I am not asking you to go back. All I ask of you is to take care of yourself. I love you."

"I love you too. We have a mess to clean up."
Finally, some light laughter returned.

Tragedy kept me from work but didn't stop our debtors from wanting their money. Ed knew my parents, family, and the volunteers would take care of me, so out of pure necessity, he returned to work. I might not be alone but I felt as if I were.

My soul is in anguish.
How long, O LORD, how long?
Psalm 6:3

CHAPTER 13

A time to kill...
Ecclesiastes 3:3a

Exhaustion and grief consumed my heart, mind, and body. The physical and mental strain became an invisible weight on my shoulders. I was exhausted but unable to sleep. It was easy to get lost in the crowd.

One day I passed a mirror, my reflection mirrored the deep sorrow and emptiness I saw in my parents' eyes. My attempts to hide my stress failed.

Heidi's disappearance was a learning experience with no local precedent case for law enforcement to rely on or a how-to book for the family. The uniqueness of Heidi's kidnapping demanded everyone think differently.

We needed to think beyond our means and utilize whatever we could if Heidi was to be found. Over one hundred searchers flooded the NHVFD that first day to ignite an awe-inspiring momentum, one that invited media coverage.

Press Conferences

Various locations, times, and reasons forced my parents from their protected seclusion to face cameras, microphones, and questions from the media.

The media plays a vital part in any kidnapping case. They have influential power with their viewing audience to either help or hinder a case. As the parents or sibling of the missing, it is common to have cameras following you in hopes to get a break or the front-page byline.

My parents strove to keep the cameras and media at bay throughout the case to protect me from their sometimes hurtful and painful questions. I listened to my parents respond, always intrigued at their ability to stay focused with little emotion while in front of the cameras.

I cringed with each "Mr. and Mrs. Allen, how does it feel to have your daughter kidnapped?" *How do you think it feels, buddy? How would you feel if someone stole your child? You get upset if someone takes your front row seat for the conference.* I wanted to jump to my parents' defense.

The LORD is close to the brokenhearted
And saves those who are crushed in spirit.
A righteous man may have many troubles,
But the LORD delivers him from them all...
Psalm 34:18-19

My protection was not necessary. Mom and Dad calmly responded: "I don't know how to put our feelings into words and I hope you never are in the same position."

I remember asking my Mom, "How do you respond so calmly as if they asked you about the weather?"

Dad answered for her, "Each interview is an opportunity to have Heidi's picture and information released to the community and beyond. Every time her picture and the phone number are seen, the more likely we are to find her." I developed a new appreciation and respect for my parents.

My parents' rapport with the media, along with their ability to suppress their emotions was an inspiration to those watching. *How did they do it?* I envied their strength.

Reflection

I felt shut out and excluded from the process of finding Heidi. I understood they lost a daughter but I lost my best friend and only sister. I understood their loss was great and couldn't imagine their pain or grief, but on the other hand, no one ever asks: "How is Heidi's sister doing?" It is always: "How are her parents? I don't know how they do it."

I didn't want to be leading a press conference, but at the same time, I wanted someone to understand, recognize me, and someone to ask me how I am doing. Did anyone realize there is more to Heidi than her parents? I felt if I acknowledged these feelings, I would sound selfish, unloving toward my sister, and disrespectful to my parents.

These were neither selfish nor unloving thoughts, but instead thoughts that kept me from accepting her disappearance and starting the process of healing. It was difficult to watch my parents each time they talked about their feelings and experiences while I ached for just one person to recognize that the sibling suffers too.

A parent and child have a special bond, just as siblings have a special bond that keep them close. I lost my sister and no one seemed to care. I recognized that a parent's loss is more prominent and newsworthy but the loss of a sibling is real and life changing.

My parents never knew how I felt because I didn't tell them. It was not until my Mom read the first draft of this book that they knew how I felt so many years ago. My parents apologized for hurting my feelings and explained their reason for keeping me on the sidelines.

With tears in my eyes, I assured them, "I know this, Mom. This is how I felt then."

Mom understood. She said, "But you should have told us."

"Mom, you were doing what you needed to do and thought was best. My feelings were insignificant, finding Heidi was the priority."

"No, both of our girls' safety and well-being are, and were important. We wish you told us. We are so sorry. Will you ever forgive us?"

"Mom, Dad…there is nothing to forgive. I do not feel this way now. Deep down, I think I always knew why, but it still hurt. I am sorry for making you feel bad when you read my draft. It was never my intention to hurt you." My heart ached for the pain I caused more than ten years later.

Inevitably, it was a blessing because our bond was stronger due to this miscommunication. The irony of the matter was that I didn't want to be in front of the cameras, but wanted the option to decide for myself.

The words of the reckless pierce like swords,
But the tongue of the wise brings healing.
Proverbs 12:18

Sara Anne Wood Center **Provides Assistance**

In addition to local volunteers and the media, the *Sara Anne Wood Center* sent a representative on Easter Sunday too. The volunteer offered suggestions and a willingness to help. In the days that followed, they printed and disseminated around 10,000 missing person's flyers of Heidi across the country too.

On Monday afternoon, Robert Wood, Sara's father, used the Sheriff's hotline number and called my mother. Mr. Wood took the time to let my parents know he and his search center were an available resource. Both he and his wife understood all too well, how my parents felt.

Mom's face relaxed as she listened, a slight quiver on her lips. The reality of a living nightmare, shared from one parent to another, touched her deeply. She returned the receiver to its resting position. My father wrapped her in his loving embrace as if no one were watching.

My parents held each other, tears gently trickling down their cheeks, a picture of love, loss, and security forever etched in my brain. It was a picture of unity in the midst of separation. I don't know if others witnessed this tender moment but the center's atmosphere changed after that phone call. A renewed hope and drive flowed through the room. *Or was it something more, had my perspective changed?*

You hear, O LORD, the desire of the afflicted;
You encourage them, and you listen to their cry.
Psalm 10:17

Missing Person Fliers

Later that day, about fifty people walked the roadsides for the one-square mile surrounding the convenience store in hopes of finding any small clue that would help the investigation. Their attention, directed toward the ground. Local print shops and businesses donated copy machines, paper, and other necessities to help with the search.

The New Haven volunteer firefighters took shifts standing in the center of Route 104 handing out flyers. A two-sided easel, propped next to them echoed their heart's message: "Pray for Heidi's Return." Each flyer was, and is, a tactile message of hope from our community to passersby.

April fifth was a dark day for the search. Volunteers returned from the field and all searches stopped. The number of volunteers was sporadic and exhaustion replaced adrenaline for all involved. The volunteers worked, searched, and functioned on pure adrenaline of love. The Sheriff and my parents didn't want to stop looking for Heidi, yet no one could fathom the thought of someone getting hurt in the process. *We can't stop. Doesn't anyone understand?*

Dad squeezed me into his side. "Kid, I don't want anyone else hurt or missing. We have to stop. Just momentarily, so everyone can get some rest."

"I'm not sleeping, I have to do something," I said as I moved away.

Inside, the efforts to find Heidi continued. Volunteers worked around the clock to copy and prepare Heidi's missing person flyer for distribution. An assembly line developed as reams of white paper transformed into black and white copies displaying Heidi's face and information.

The copiers printed hundreds of flyers per hour. I prayed the volunteers could keep up. I offered to help once again but was sent back to my corner "…to relax, blah, blah, blah". It was the same story I heard repeatedly.

Stubborn, bored, and nervous -- I picked up a stack of newly printed flyers. I cradled the still warm pages in my hands as I walked over to a table in the "copy center." I didn't ask permission. I simply sat down with a fierce determination to help.

In a soft voice, someone explained, "All right Lisa, place this cover letter on top of twenty to twenty-five flyers and then place it in one of these envelopes. Stack the stuffed envelopes in the box labeled, "need addresses". Someone will empty the box when it is full. Lisa…do you hear me?"

Of course I heard you, was I not sitting here staring at you and smiling? This is not brain surgery. Let me get to work.

I worked joyously at first to count pages, drop on the cover sheet, and slide each stack into an envelope. Then as abruptly as I joined the effort, the young girl staring at me from the flyer entranced me. *Oh my gosh, that is my sister.* I apologized, excused myself and retreated to my corner, on my own accord that time.

Thankfully, my departure didn't stop the process. I watched from afar. So this was why I am left on the sidelines, I was incapable. The filled envelopes moved to the next table for addresses.

Initially, we didn't have pre-printed address labels available so volunteers spent countless hours, handwriting the names of town clerks and police stations across the United States and Canada. Volunteers divided the finished envelopes into bins labeled "local", "out-of-state", "Syracuse", and "UPS".

Wayne Cowley and Ed Stevens brought the overflowing white postal service bins to the New Haven Post Office multiple times a day. With multiple trips each day they swapped out full bins for empty ones. A UPS driver graciously stopped each afternoon as a courtesy to save the forty-minute drive one-way to deliver the newly stuffed envelopes.

Would someone recognize her face and call? Would someone who witnessed her abduction see the flyer and call? We could only HOPE it was not wasted ink.

The constant, monotonous swoosh of the copier began to lull me to sleep. I fought to stay awake. What if they found Heidi and I was sleeping? How disappointed she would be. *What would Heidi think of me if I chose to sleep instead of search?* Forty-eight hours and 20,000 missing person's flyers later, we were overcome with weariness. Sleep deprivation caused feelings of confusion.

Exhausted and In Need of Help

In order to maintain sanity and functionality within the center, reinforcements were necessary. This required my parents or me to leave the command center,unthinkable. Our fears confined us within the four walls so someone else would need to step up. I was thankful for my family's ability to think and reason since this was a skill I found difficult, if not impossible, then.

...But we also rejoice in our sufferings,

Because we know that

Suffering produces perseverance;

Perseverance, character;

And character, hope.

And hope does not disappoint us,

Because God has poured out his love

Into our hearts by the Holy Spirit,

Whom he has given us.

Romans 5:3-5

CHAPTER 14

And a time to heal...
Ecclesiastes 3:3a

Family, friends, and community members
remained with us non-stop. Auntie M and Unc left
the command center determined to find the help we
desperately needed. I didn't see them leave because
my focus was on my own loss. *When did they go out?*
Where are they coming from? Did I doze off? Oh no, I let
Heidi down.

Their return was dramatic, gliding through the
door while voicing, "Where are Ken and Sue?" They
didn't wait for a response but instead scanned the
room themselves. *Had Heidi been found? Was her body*
found? Was this nightmare finally over? I dared to hope.

Excitement transitioned to despair as I
contemplated what was happening. Conflicting
thoughts swirled through my head. Was Heidi alive?
For the first time it dawned on me that I might never
see my sister alive again.

I watched my aunt and uncle's mouths move a
mile a minute as they shared their news. The
anticipation was too much so I stood up and started

across the room. I stopped midway. Maybe if I didn't go over, my fears wouldn't become reality. I walked.

As I walked, my eyes shifted to my parents. Each bore a contemplative look. I stopped. It was evident it was not the message I longed to hear. The Sheriff joined the discussion.

My aunt and uncle smiled, then as swiftly as they entered, they exited without a word. *What was going on? Could someone please explain?*

Entranced by the scene that unfolded before my eyes, my parents walked over and guided me back to the family corner. Before I could formulate a question, they began to share what transpired.

"Your aunt and uncle have found a search and rescue expert," Mom said.

"He works with a center in Texas specializing in finding missing persons," Dad added.

Mom placed her finger on my lips. "We need his expertise, Lisa. We have to do this."

"It is going to be okay. Lisa, are you okay? Lisa?" My Dad's words were lost but the warmth of his hands on my shoulders warmed my heart and helped me to believe this was good.

The news was not a joyous announcement of Heidi's recovery, but it was cause for celebration.

Mom and Dad seemed hopeful. I wished I could share their enthusiasm.

Expertise with a Texan Twist

While Auntie M and Unc made flight arrangements and found a place for him to stay while in New York, Mom and Dad shared with me what they learned. I don't know the word or words used to "search" the Internet for help, but it must have included the name "Heidi".

The *Heidi Search Center* located in San Antonio, Texas was the first site listed. The man they spoke with was Rick, Director of Missing Persons & Chief Operations. He shared the ninety-seven percent success rate with their center, and he would personally make the trip the following day if my parents were interested.

The *Heidi Search Center,* established after eleven-year-old Heidi Seeman was kidnapped while walking home from her friend's house on August 4, 1990. Heidi Seeman was their first case. Heidi Allen would be their forty-second case, and only the third from outside the state of Texas. The only cost to the family was for his travel, housing, and food expenses.

Auntie M and Unc provided the airfare. Uncle Tom and Aunt Linda let him stay at a vacant rental property and he ate with our family and the volunteers at the *Heidi Allen Search Center*. With the particulars in order, the only thing to do was wait upon his arrival. Wait...something I was tired of doing.

It had only been four days – four days that felt like an eternity. Rick arrived on April 7. He came in with an expertise and gift for administration and delegation. He was able to make decisions too difficult for family members to deal with and he worked with the Sheriff's investigators, FBI, and the hundreds of volunteers simultaneously.

Rick complimented the organization and search efforts developed prior to his arrival. He was impressed with the number of contacts and flyers already circulating.

I marveled at this man strolling through the door with his Texan hat and cowboy boots. Tall, thin, and tanned, he walked with an air of confidence.

Auntie M and Unc led the way, and it was apparent he learned the details of Heidi's case during his ride from the airport. He was introduced to my parents first and then to the Sheriff and his team. Within moments, he called a meeting.

My admiration turned to frustration. *Who did this guy think he was? We had been here non-stop for over three days, working 24/7. His audacity irritated me.* My face betrayed my thoughts. My husband wrapped his arm around me.

"Lisa, he is doing his job. He is the search expert. If he doesn't know all the details then he and this investigation won't move forward. Give him a chance." He was right, of course, but still I couldn't help feeling insecure in his abilities.

Once the initial meeting concluded, my parents brought this man over to meet Ed and me. I reached out my hand and found myself scooped into a hug instead. "Texans hug," he said with a smile. With his high success rate, and his Texas-sized confidence, I knew he would find Heidi. The odds were in our favor, right?

But just as quickly, doubts swirled through my mind once again. What if Heidi was one of the three-percent never found? I didn't know...so I chose to believe he WOULD find her. Within moments, Rick strode across the room introducing himself to all the volunteers, and calling more meetings.

As I watched him work the room and finalize the transformation of the "Heidi Allen Command Center", I was suddenly exhausted. I needed a nap. I needed to sleep. Rick, determined and resourceful, provided a renewed hope and energy to the search. He came in, recognized the areas of weakness, and made the necessary changes without worrying about hurt feelings. He didn't come to New York to make friends. He had one goal and purpose: to find Heidi.

"Come to me, all you who are weary and burdened,
And I will give you rest.
Take my yoke upon you and learn from me,
For I am gentle and humble in heart,
And you will find rest for your souls."
Matthew 11:28 – 29

CHAPTER 15

A time to tear down…
Ecclesiastes 3:3b

A Look Back to Rick's Arrival

Rick, our new missing person's expert, sauntered through the door on Thursday afternoon. To our tired team, his expertise and positive outlook were a blessing.

He shook each person's hand with a, "Hi, I'm Rick. Glad to meet you."

His eyes scanned the room from one side to the other while he introduced himself. He examined the center and everyone there in the process, clever.

He stated the obvious: "Heidi Allen has been missing for four days and each minute she is missing – the less likely we are to see her again." As if this wasn't hard enough to listen to, at times he even broke it down to the exact number of hours. It was a constant reminder of how valuable one minute can be when someone you love is missing.

Rick knew this and saw the strength and potential in our community. "I'm here to enhance a well-oiled machine. With your heart and my expertise, we will find Heidi."

I started to believe him. Rick's fast pace and constant follow-up kept everyone on his or her toes. His energy infiltrated a tired community's heart and restored hope. It felt good to smile again, to have warmth in my heart rather than the chill of grief. If only it lasted.

> *I will lead the blind by ways they have not known,*
> *Along unfamiliar paths I will guide them;*
> *I will turn darkness into light before them*
> *And make the rough places smooth.*
> *These are the things I will do;*
> *I will not forsake them.*
> Isaiah 42:16

A Painful Change

"Ken. I need to talk to you, Sue, and the Sheriff for a minute. Can you come with me?" With a nod, Mom and Dad stood to join Rick.

Auntie M and Unc started to follow until Rick said, "No, only Ken and Sue." *Who did this guy think he was? We are a family, a team. My parents need us.*

Mom raised her hand, as if to say, "It's okay, we'll be right back." Frustrated, Auntie M and Unc went outside. I merely stood. He'd just met me. He knew Heidi had a sister. I didn't know if I should be angry or hurt.

While I struggled with the reality of my exclusion, I was glad to know my parents had some relief. There was hope. *Thank goodness the Lord brought Rick to my aunt and uncle's attention.* I wondered if there were more changes coming?

In reality, there probably wasn't anything shared in private we wouldn't have eventually heard, but I viewed it as a lack of trust instead of validity for the case. *Could I not simply have joined my parents and heard it firsthand? I was twenty-three years old, I could handle it. Couldn't I?*

Instead of thinking of my parents' needs, it was about me. I wanted to be with and near them, not on the sidelines with everyone else. They were my security, something I needed at that time.

Rick cupped his hands in front of his mouth. "Volunteers make your way to the center tables. While you gather everyone from outside, I'm want to meet with the immediate family. I'll be right over."

Changes Revealed

My parents, and Rick, revealed their private conversation. Immediate changes WERE necessary to secure the center and enhance the search efforts. *Why did we need so much change?* He had only been in town for a few hours and was already changing our "well-oiled machine". After that welcoming hug, I thought he would be different.

With my husband's arm wrapped around my shoulders, I listened in anticipation. Dad started. "For the remainder of the case, all new information will be filtered through us, to you."

While others appeared unsettled by this, a sense of smugness crept in. I would not be the only one left out from now on.

Aunt Nancy sat to my other side, leaned in and said, "It will be all right, don't worry." *Do I look worried?* Surrounded by aunts, uncles, cousins, and Heidi's boyfriend Brett, I watched my parents' faces as they spoke. Something was missing in their expressions, but what?

Dad winked at me before starting. "Thank you again for all you are doing and have done. We could not do this without each of you. From delivering missing person's fliers to contacting the media." As Dad said the word "we", he motioned to mom, himself, Ed, and me. *Maybe they hadn't forgotten me completely, so why did I doubt their love?*

He continued. "From this moment forward we each have a different role to play." Auntie M and Unc looked confused by this announcement, mouthing a conversation between them. My cousins' eyebrows rose with an inquisitive, almost shocked look on their faces.

Before anyone could interrupt, Mom picked up where Dad left off. "We are still working as a team to find Heidi, but under Rick's guidance and leadership. This is why he is here. We need to let him do his job."

Dad explained: "Rick will choose volunteers to coordinate the different areas within the center, so we, the family, can focus on finding Heidi. This also increases the integrity and validity of the case, while controlling the information released to the public."

We entered the family corner unified, but after this conversation, the hurt feelings and confusion caused a divide. Rick never said a word, just listened and watched our reactions.

Mom interjected: "We appreciate everything you each have done for us and Heidi, but Rick advised us to tighten the core. This isn't personal. Your hard work, dedication, and support keep us going and have helped to develop a well-run center..."

Dad finished her sentence. "...But we've all reached our limits. Rick and the sheriff's department will lead our decision-making from now on. They are the experts." *Go Mom and Dad.*

"Business isn't personal, it's purposeful." We were a business. *When did this happen? Their daughter was missing, this was VERY personal.* Mom leaned into Dad. They exchanged a glance of hope and relief. Fighting back tears, unable to even say "thank you", they walked toward the private entrance, leaning on each other for support.

How long, O LORD?
Will you forget me forever?
How long will you hide your face from me?
How long must I wrestle with my thoughts
And every day have sorrow in my heart?
How long will my enemy triumph over me?
Psalm 13:1-2

CHAPTER 16

And a time to build...
Ecclesiastes 3:3b

Rick's Purpose and Mission

Local media spread the word of Rick's arrival and the need for more volunteers. Rick welcomed each new and returning volunteer with a smile.

He stood tall, taking his hat off when he spoke. "While New Haven is new to me, a missing person isn't. The new division of responsibility allows law enforcement to focus on the investigation, not the volunteers."

I'm glad I came over and heard him speak. He cared and it *was* still personal, it was just a different way of doing things.

I overheard volunteers talking and was amazed at the impact Rick had in such a short amount of time. "If they're going to find Heidi, this is the guy who can do it."

Wow. In less than fifteen minutes, he'd won over the community. *But what if he didn't find her?*

Rick's next statement snapped me out of my daze. "There is an eighteen year old girl missing."

Is he kidding? Did he think we'd forgotten? Maybe his coming wasn't a good idea after all. I didn't know if it was he, or I, in need of more explanation.

Rick's voice intensified and I listened with anticipation until I heard what he started to say, "...more than half the cases."

I recognized this phrase, even while I didn't want to hear it. I remained with the group out of curiosity. *Maybe he would say something different; was the officer wrong earlier? Would it be a more hopeful message this time?*

With compassion in his voice, Rick continued. "...more than half the cases utilizing community search teams will have the abductor searching alongside good-hearted people like yourselves. Most likely the abductor is one of your neighbors or standing next to you at this moment."

You could have heard a pin drop in the room.

Nausea settled in, my knees weakened, and I could feel my face start to flush. I needed to sit down. Why did people keep saying this? Things like this didn't happen in New Haven.

But it did happen, Heidi was missing, and we were searching.

~ 126 ~

If this could happen, then it only made sense the remaining statistics could happen too. My wonderful and once safe small town was only a mirage. *If the kidnappers were local, why would they join in the search, wouldn't they already know where the body was?* I still didn't understand. Why? I was tired of listening, tired of thinking, and most importantly, tired of waiting. *Would it ever end?*

We were searching for one person, but Heidi was Rick's sixth case in the past three months. He instantly recognized the tension and the dark circles shadowing everyone's eyes. He searched for half a dozen missing persons. Why didn't he appear tired? I wanted to go home and sleep in my own bed but couldn't fathom the thought of leaving the center. I hoped he would share his secret with us.

One of my parents' concerns was Rick's first observation: "Your family is emotionally drained and the entire search team is minutes from burnout." After ninety-six hours of working on adrenaline, Rick's leadership relieved some of the stress and provided a much-needed break.

In spite of Rick's involvement, I struggled to remain hopeful. I looked him straight in the eyes before stating: "You had clues in your first "Heidi" case and in the five cases before joining us. We have nothing. My sister will be one of your 3% still missing when you board your plane for Texas." *Why did I just tell him that?* I hadn't even shared this frustration with my parents. I was glad he was there.

Tears streamed down my cheeks, my nose turned red, and my head started to pound. Rick extended his arms and pulled me in. No words, only a hug and tears.

Carry each other's burdens,
And in this way you will fulfill the law of Christ.
Galatians 6:2

Vigilantes to Experts

A determined community with Rick at the helm ensured that if there was a way to bring Heidi home, it would happen. I was surrounded by amazing people giving of themselves to find Heidi, but someone was going to get hurt. *Was there a way to focus their energy while keeping them and others safe?* Thankfully, someone else with power and a solution was paying attention too.

Rick recognized the vigilante search tactics immediately and held a private meeting outside with the searchers. In the dark of the night and in hushed tones, Rick praised them. "I haven't seen a finer group of men and women working to find a missing person, BUT you are scaring your neighbors and someone is going to get hurt. The sheriffs are fielding more calls about you than about Heidi."

There was more whispering, then silence.

After a few moments, Rick broke the silence. "The rules need to be followed. If you are willing to follow the rules, come with me."

Out of the shadows emerged recharged men and women.

When they returned inside, I overheard one man's voice. "I never meant to scare anyone. I just wanted to help."

"We all did. We were doing the best we could. Sitting idle wasn't an option. This person has the expertise to train us. We only need to be open to his suggestions." was the response.

Their concern and strong sense of community combined with Rick's special training guaranteed meaningful searches. I knew I lived in a great place. I listened to the volunteers speak as if Heidi was their sister – emotions overwhelmed me.

At 2:00 a.m. Rick shared safe and effective search techniques and guidelines. Using the sheriff's same rules, Rick raised a fist over his head and began.

With each guideline he thrust one finger from the clenched fist and pointed in the air.

"Don't handle evidence, NO night searches, NO searching of private property, NO carrying of firearms, and most importantly, stay out of the law enforcement's way." Some took notes and others simply listened.

It was vital everyone knew and understood these rules. Rick went over them multiple times. With each review, he thrust his hand into the air. Each finger represented one rule, an unspoken reminder between the searchers and their newfound leader. Our volunteers had the potential to be professionals before the sun rose.

Prior to Rick, our rural countrymen and women searched the way they hunted. They grabbed their spotlights, extra clothing, CB's and a firearm. I was confident if they found Heidi, they would have used all their expertise and heart to return her safely to my parents. Their compassion and knowledge appeared to frighten the sheriff's department and Rick.

And then there was a new obstacle: the holiday vacation ended. Searchers and volunteers expressed their sorrow for not being able to stay longer. I understood their dilemma. Their hearts desired to remain at the center but their empty cupboards and debts reminded them it was time to return to work. This obstacle weighed me down. We finally had an expert on the team but lost our support. *What next?* I shouldn't have asked. The weather became dark and dreary and brought on additional difficulties.

Challenges aside, my parents remained pillars of strength and breathtaking examples of hope. Instead of following their example, I let anger, frustration, and fear seep in. I wasn't sure how I would survive this, there I went again, "I". Thank goodness, my selfish feelings didn't slow the momentum of the case.

Now to him who is able to do immeasurably more

Than all we ask or imagine,

According to his power

That is at work within us,

To him be glory in the church

And in Christ Jesus

Throughout all generations,

Forever and ever!

Amen.

Ephesians 3:20-21

CHAPTER 17

A time to search...
Ecclesiastes 3:6a

Rick, my parents, and the Sheriff had a decision to make – to continue the search with a skeletal crew or admit defeat. Heidi was still missing and we wanted to find her, but the weather and a limited number of searchers were making it near impossible.

In spite of the April rains and remaining sand-covered snow banks, the searchers refused to leave. With strength and heart, "Resume the search.," echoed throughout the room.

Dad whispered in my ear. "An Allen does not give up. It looks like our family just got bigger." I think he was right.

"Call in the troops!" someone yelled. Fists fly into the air, cheers echoed.

Searchers, volunteers, law enforcement, and family refueled with much needed nourishment. But Rick -- he rallied my father and uncles. A comment made in jest sparked a movement. Oh my gosh. They were really calling in the troops. *Was this real? Someone pinch me.*

The Troops Arrive

My initial plan when writing this book was to include all the details leading up to, and following the military's arrival in New Haven fifteen days into the investigation. After some thought, I've decided to leave it out. While important, the exact details aren't pertinent to my story.

In all honesty, I don't remember most of the details. If it weren't for the saved newspaper clippings, the order of things would be more disorganized than it might already be. The logistics of the 27th Brigade's arrival might be monumental, especially in the history of missing persons' search efforts for New York State, but these details are not memories I can recall. *Why can I not remember? So many days, weeks and months are lost...will I ever remember?*

After rereading the newspaper articles and talking with different people, an entire chapter detailing the drama and politics involved in the recruitment and arrival are possible but not engaging for most.

I could tell you who made the contacts to have the Oswego volunteer reservists join or even the Civil Air Patrol. As if this wasn't enough, the 10th Mountain Division joined the search efforts. Is your head spinning? I know mine did and still does to this day. So many people looking for one person, why couldn't they find her?

I'm forever grateful to Rick for opening the door to show us this wasn't simply a statement made in jest, but a necessity. The men and women in camouflage walked in tall and determined from the moment they arrived. This new assignment was executed –as if it was personal. Motivation and hope filled the room.

Within two days, of "Call in the troops!", they rolled in and set up tents in the backfield. With tears in my eyes, I watched the trucks pull in. I mouthed the words "Thank you" to each passing vehicle and soldier. From a distance, they nodded their heads toward me. As they walked past me, they said: "It's our honor." *Did they know how much their being there meant to my family? To me?*

In addition to the military, there were various "search and rescue" horse teams. They searched along the creeks, roadsides, and in the fields. Who knew there were people and horses trained to work together to search for the missing? I know I didn't. *What was next?* On the other side of the fire hall were search teams utilizing dogs.

Cameras and reporters seemed to match the

number of volunteers. It was impossible to have a private moment without a camera capturing the moment for the next day's story. There were reporters and journalists from Watertown and Rochester, all there to witness history in the making. Dad told me, "This is the first time a search of this magnitude has occurred in New York, and it is all for Heidi."

So many people arrived in such a short amount of time. I buried my head in my hands and cried, hopeful and overwhelmed.

Would the soldiers and search teams be able to find Heidi? Did they say they were looking for her body? Wasn't she still alive? Would their special training finally bring Heidi home? Or was it too late?

Don't Question Authority

In light of the increased number of people circulating through the center, Rick stressed the importance of documentation. "We need a handful of people willing to make sure every person that enters that door signs in." *Was he kidding? That was a full-time job in itself. Maybe I'd be able to help now.*

Someone questioned him. "Are you serious? Is this necessary?"

Rick's response was quick and serious. "Were you listening to what I just said?"

The woman turned with tears in her eyes as

she spoke. "I'm sorry. I just..." *A bit harsh.* We all understood, and his point, made. Other volunteers didn't question or wait but went to work. This woman looked to Rick, "Where do you want me?"

Pat, Betty, and Ann set-up a registration table near the door. One gathered signatures of those already in the room while the other made sure each person entering knew of our new protocol. Wow, things were changing fast.

Questions flooded my brain. I didn't know if I ever voiced them but they were continuous within my own head. My emotions transitioned from hopeful to despair on a moment's notice.

Conversations surrounded me but were never directly to me. I overheard one of the searchers say, "We found a pair of jeans." Rick's radio broadcast loud enough for all to hear: "Team two found a pair of glasses similar to the teen's."

Although only minutes passed, it felt like hours before we learned they belonged to someone else. *We were never going to find her. Why God, why? I hate you. I want my sister back. Don't you care?*

Miscellaneous items left behind as litter became symbols of hope, potential evidence, and stressors. I never knew a pair of jeans left in the woods could create such emotion. A white canvas sneaker, glasses, or a hair scrunchy might be the one clue to bring Heidi home.

If only something fell or ripped during her struggle, or wherever they took her, we might have a clue.

Who of you by worrying can
Add a single hour to your life?
Luke 12:25

CHAPTER 18

And a time to give up...
Ecclesiastes 3:6a

What is my purpose?

Each day, and search, was another twist and turn of the emotional roller coaster called my life. I felt isolated. Isolation transitioned into anger. You might be thinking, "How can you feel alone if there are hundreds of volunteers, searchers, and family members surrounding you?" I learned that just because people are around you, doesn't mean you have company.

The people passing by me had a purpose, to find Heidi. My purpose was to sit and wait. *Why did no one think I could help?* There is danger in spending time lost in your thoughts. I learned irrational and negative thoughts had a better chance to infiltrate an already tired and lonely heart.

Everyone had a task and knew how to get it done. I felt as if the only thing I could do was sit, wait and watch. I was angered with whoever took Heidi. Bitterness and frustration crept in each time I tried to help. Instead of doing something, I returned to my seat in the corner.

Was I a new puppy? Punished for having an accident on the floor? Bad Lisa, go to your corner.

I misconstrued the compassion and love expressed as punishment. *Should I have told someone how I was feeling?* Instead of sharing my feelings, I buried them deep within myself so no one could see, or so I thought.

My attempt to hide my true feelings actually created a barrier. The raw emotions of inner turmoil and anger didn't stay hidden but appeared in the other areas of my life. The wellspring of my life had run dry and I wasn't looking for a repair.

Above all else, guard your heart,
For it is the wellspring of life.
Proverbs 4:23

The irony, I found satisfaction in being miserable. I said and did things I knew would cause pain to others. Instead of embracing suffering, I relished my ability to inflict hurt to others. I had no interest in a God who allowed my eighteen-year-old sister to be kidnapped.

If God truly existed, then why did he take my sister? If He wasn't the one that took Heidi, then why pray to a God that could have prevented this in the first place?

Questions fueled my frustration.

A German shepherd's bark startled me back to reality. Hundreds of people came and went, each with a specific goal or mission. I found myself on the back stoop off the kitchen, watching the search teams prepare their dogs for another mission. I marveled at the relationship between master and dog. I missed my sister. How did the dogs know what or who to smell?

A lesson learned

Heidi lived with our Gram Mary and Aunt Nancy prior to her kidnapping. Gram needed to keep busy while she waited. Usually when under stress, Gram baked, but because it was Easter Sunday, the oven was full of ham, potatoes, and stuffing. Gram headed upstairs to clean Heidi's room.

When Aunt Nancy returned, Gram said, "I stripped Heidi's bed and washed all the bedding and all her clothes from her hamper."

"Mom, you shouldn't have done that."

With her worry and Irish temper triggered, "What do you want me to do? Just sit here? When they find Heidi she will want to sleep and she can do it on clean sheets."

"But, Mom…"

"But nothing. Plus, I don't want the sheriff's investigators to see her room messy or her

~ 141 ~

undergarments lying around. What would they think?" *She was always thinking.*

"You're right Mom. Great thinking. I'm heading back to the center, call if you need me."

How do the dogs know what to smell? Do you remember this question? The answer is simple. They sniff the dirty clothing and bedding of the missing.

Each time we lay our heads on our pillow or fill our hampers with dirty clothes, the perfume of our DNA remains. Once washed, the smells and DNA vanish, just like our missing loved one. Cleanliness is a luxury until it interferes with a search and rescue mission.

What would the dogs use now? I watched one of the dog teams and realized the dogs were sniffing the inside of someone's sneakers, Heidi's sneakers to be exact. Would it be enough to give them a scent?

Little did I know at the time, some of the dog teams were using Heidi's sneakers and jackets to pick up a scent, while others were cadaver teams. I didn't know what this meant but was thankful they knew what to sniff.

"The cadaver team found something." echoed through the multitude of radios attached to law enforcement and the team leader's hips.

Excitement came over me until I heard my

mother. "I have to sit down."

Confused, I joined my Mom. She read my mind. "Lisa, do you know what a cadaver is?"

"No, but isn't it good that they found something?"

"Lisa, a cadaver is a dead body. The dog team found a dead body."

Excitement mutated into nausea. They found Heidi's body. *Should I be happy or sad?* I chose somber. We sat and waited.

With muffled conversation and the tick-tock of the clock, finally there was more information. "False alarm. Repeat, false alarm. These are not human remains."

Echoes came from each walkie-talkie. Relief...it isn't Heidi. There was still hope. Or should I have hoped it was her? Either way, the outcome ripped at my heart.

I watched another search team prepare to depart. The woman appeared motivated to return to the search. What drives someone to continue to search? Did they realize they might be the one to find Heidi's body, or was this why they did it?

Fast Forward Ten Years to November 2004

I thought God abandoned me, but instead He surrounded me with His love. Hopeless and searching, God used a child's simple request to restore hope with my phone call to the pastor and a promise kept. I walked through the doors of Community Alliance Church. I was instantly welcomed with open arms and with such love I knew I found a church I could call home.

There were so many new faces. One seemed more familiar than the rest. "Do I know you?"

"I don't think so. My name is Burnetta."

Nearly a Year After This Meeting ~ September 2005

Each year on Heidi's birthday, I watched old home movies and media clips about her disappearance. I had my tissues ready, hit play, and the day began. Oh my gosh, I know her. I could not believe my reddened eyes. I recognized one of the searchers, Burnetta. I knew she looked familiar. Why didn't she say anything? Should I? God didn't leave much time for me to worry about it, and the following Sunday, Burnetta wore her "Search and Rescue" jacket to church.

"Burnetta, can I ask you a question?"

With a smile on her face, she said, "Yes."

"I don't know how to ask this, but…"

She interrupted my staggered response. "I said yes. Yes, I was on the search and rescue teams for your sister."

I was speechless as tears welled in my eyes. "Thank you."

Thankful for her willingness to search and overwhelmed by God's provision when I thought He was nowhere to be found. I asked, "Why didn't you tell me?"

Wiping tears from her eyes too, she said, "I knew when you were ready, you would remember, make the connection, and approach me."

As we talked she shared her prayer, for us to become better friends first and then for me realize we had met before. She trusted the Lord and let me come to her and I trusted the Lord as I approached her. I am thankful the Lord brought her into my life. She is a blessing.

Trust in the LORD *with all your heart*

And lean not on your own understanding;

In all your ways submit to him,

And he will make your paths straight.

Proverbs 2:5-6

CHAPTER 19

A time to love...
Ecclesiastes 3:8a

Flashback to 1994 Again

Our community extended their hands, hearts, and love to my family daily. In the moments they weren't helping with the search, volunteering, baking, or cooking; they were planning, preparing, and organizing.

I couldn't remember if I put on deodorant, but these men and women still had the ability to use their brains, thank goodness. With the center running smoothly and everyone's tummies full, other nourishment was needed, that of our souls. A candlelight vigil was planned.

Thus far in the investigation I was told, "No, we can do it." Or, "Thanks but we're all set" each time I offered to help. As the notion of holding a candlelight vigil developed, I found encouragement. Surely they would let me help plan an event like this?

I went to church, I prayed, and it would give me something to do. More importantly, it would get me out of their way for a little while. I was going to volunteer. The vigil offered a new opportunity for me to assist in the efforts to find Heidi.

"Mom, is there something I can do to help with the candlelight vigil?" I asked.

Mom smiled and nodded. "Of course, why couldn't you?"

"I don't know. I just wanted to ask." *Should I have told her that I felt like the only thing I was told when I offered to help was "No"? No, I wouldn't tell her; she had enough to worry about.*

I left my mom and joined the ladies to plan for the first vigil. I was so excited. "Hi, can I help? I checked with my mom, she is okay with it." *Please don't say no, please, please.*

"Of course you can. That will be nice. Who would know what music and Bible verses Heidi likes better than her own sister?" *Not only could I help, but I could select the music. Yes.*

To honor all religious backgrounds, the vigil was held in the side yard of the NHVFC. Pastor Vivian, of the New Haven United Methodist Church was invited to lead this time of prayer and remembrance.

The vigil restored more than my hope. It reminded me I had talents and what I could do to help bring my sister home. I had a purpose once again and I hoped it would last. The vigil was going to be beautiful. The songs were selected, the candles and cups purchased, the media notified, and the music was ready. We waited for the afternoon to darken to evening. For the first time in days, I didn't mind waiting.

Music greeted everyone through the speakers on either side of the fire department's front sign. Vehicles lined both sides of State Route 104 and filled the parking lot. The community, family, friends, and the media arrived in numbers greater than I had anticipated.

Parents with young children, grandparents, off-duty law enforcement investigators, and officers. offered their condolences as they received their candles and found a spot to stand. Volunteers walked through the crowd to ensure everyone had a candle, even the kids.

I was overcome with emotion. Eric Clapton's words captured my thoughts. *Would I see Heidi again? Alive? Or would I have to wait until I die?* Questions took my thoughts captive. Pastor Vivian's voice interrupted my thoughts, and I realized the music stopped and she was opening with a prayer.

The vigil was underway.

"On behalf of the family, I want to thank you all for coming. Let us open with a word of prayer. Dear Lord..." It was silent; the only sound was Pastor Vivian's voice and muffled sobs from the crowd. I didn't think I could stand there without crying. *Would anyone notice if I sneaked back inside until it was over?* I thought Ed could read my mind.

"Lisa, it is okay to cry. Let it out. I'm right here." Ed reassured me while holding me up.

A sense of calm replaced the chaos and busyness. People traveled from across the county and beyond to join in prayer for Heidi's safe return. *Where were all these people coming from? Why were they here?* That one fact made me want to cry.

As I scanned the crowd, I noticed some of Heidi's friends from Bishop Cunningham, friends of my parents, the volunteers with their families at their side, people from church, and more. A tiny voice caught my attention.

My little cousin, K.C. was helping to hand out candles. "Thank you for coming." *I wonder if he understood where Heidi was? Or if he understood what happened?*

There were so many people gathered to light candles of hope and unite in prayer. The vigil was a success and we planned more in the future. The weather didn't deter people from attending the vigils. One evening it was so cold and damp, I was convinced no one was going to join us to stand in such horrific April weather. Boy, was I wrong. Another large turnout. I was so thankful for our community. Did they know what a blessing they were to us? Would I ever be able to thank them all?

That one particular evening, the weather caused everyone to arrive with jackets, gloves and even hats to keep them warm. T-shirts bearing Heidi's missing person's flyer were worn atop our coats and with the candles ready – we were ready to get started.

Ed pulled out his matches to light our candles so we could help light Heidi's way home. Only two matches were left – Ed lit our candles only to have the breeze blow them out.

"I only have one match left, block the wind," Ed instructed.

I tried, but as with any northeasterly upstate New York wind, it swirled about us and our match didn't have a chance. At this rate we'd have the only two unlit candles there. As if on cue, the person to my left gently leaned in to share her candlelight. With cupped hands, we lit the candles.

With a nod, tears formed in her eyes. I didn't recognize her. Her sadness and tears triggered a stream of tears of my own. I squeezed her hand with a quiet, "Thank you," before our attention returned to the speaker. Wow, it almost looked like daylight, there were so many candles. The traffic traveling State Route 104 slowed to admire the scene. Some even stopped and joined us.

"Ed, why are all these people here?"

"Heidi is a good person and your family is wonderful. It is an opportunity for the community to reach out and show their support. At least that is my idea."

"Hold me, Ed. Just hold me." I let the weight of the world rest on my husband's shoulders instead of my own, or God's.

I was lost too, just like my sister.

Setting Aside One's Feelings

Each person extended words of hope, prayers and encouragement as they passed the family. I stepped out from Ed's embrace to see Mrs. Teifke and her daughter Lisa walking toward me. They were arm in arm, leaning on each other for support as they wiped tears from their eyes with the shreds that remained of their tissues.

Oh my goodness, they were here. Mrs. Teifke lost her son, and Lisa, her brother. This must have been so hard for them. I didn't know what to say. I didn't have time to formulate the words as Mrs. Teifke wrapped her arms around me in one of the tightest hugs I had in days.

"Your family is always in our prayers." She wept as she pulled back enough to look me square in the eyes.

"Thank y..." is all I could say.

Another set of arms joined the embrace. Lisa shared our hug and tears.

The tears subsided, and with a nervous laugh we released our grip. Mrs. Teifke shared the song "Tears in Heaven" was played at her son's funeral.

Oh my goodness. The first decision I made in days and I reminded this wonderful woman of her son's funeral. Man, I blew it. I couldn't even help with the vigils without messing up.

I appeared to be listening as they each shared the significance of the song, but all I could do is beat myself up for causing them additional pain. I was not helping again. I would return to my corner until Heidi was found.

"I'm sorry. I didn't know. Can you forgive me? I didn't know. I just thought..." is all I could think to say.

"Oh my goodness, Lisa, don't apologize." Mrs. Teifke hugged me again.

"Lisa, this was healing and while it is sad – we remembered my brother again with both joy and sadness. You didn't know," Lisa added.

"I will make sure the song isn't used again. You are nice enough to come, the least I can do is make sure a different song is played. I'm sor..." and my tears returned with a vengeance.

"Don't worry about it. Tears are healthy," Mrs. Teifke said. *Then we must be three healthy ladies, living in one healthy community. All I heard was crying.*

In the Bible, a letter written by the apostle John says to not love with words or tongue but with "actions in truth". Mrs. Teifke and her daughter, Lisa loved me.

It was a love I needed at that moment, one we all need at some point in our life.

Love must be sincere.

Hate what is evil;

Cling to what is good.

Be devoted to one another in love.

Honor one another above yourselves.

Never be lacking in zeal,

But keep your spiritual fervor,

Serving the Lord.

Be joyful in hope,

Patient in affliction,

Faithful in prayer.

Share with the Lord's people

Who are in need.

Practice hospitality.

Romans 12:9-13

CHAPTER 20

And a time to hate...
Ecclesiastes 3:8a

The Candlelight Fades

A month into the investigation, the *Heidi Allen Command Center* was moved from the NHVFC to the intersection of State Route 104 and County Route 6, the center of our town.

On May 6, to commemorate the center's new home, another candlelight vigil occurred. Pastor Vivian opened the vigil in prayer as she had many times in the past, but this time I didn't stay to hear the closing prayer.

An event designed to restore hope ended up being the devil's catalyst to turn me away from God.

The warm spring breeze refreshed Ed and I as we walked the mile plus to attend the vigil. We held hands, with moments of silence and intermittent conversation.

"Ed, I never thought we would still be looking and praying for Heidi to be found a month later. I kept praying this was all a mistake, knowing it isn't, but hoping...dreaming." Tears trickled down my cheeks.

"I know. This has been the longest month of my life." He released his hand and wrapped his arm around me.

"Do you think anyone will be at the vigil? It's been so long, will the community still remember Heidi?" *Lord, let there be people there. Please don't let them forget Heidi.*

"Lisa, I hear the music. We need to walk faster."

"Okay."

Mom welcomed everyone, "Thank you for coming. We never thought..." How did she do it? Mom was so strong. I was happy to blend in with the crowd tonight. Mom remained a constant example of strength and hope.

Pastor Vivian opened with a prayer for Heidi's safe return and His protection for Heidi and the family. A prayer lifted as encouragement created turmoil and ignited my buried frustration, anger, and disappointment.

To personalize the prayer, Pastor Vivian named family members and Heidi's boyfriend by name, with a special prayer for each one. She started with my parents, and now she was praying for Brett. *What about me? Maybe I was next.*

I listened as she concluded her prayer for the family with an extensive prayer for Brett's turmoil. There was still no mention of me, Heidi's sister. I felt a knot in my throat build and my breathing deepen. With my eyebrows raised, I looked to Ed. *Please tell me she didn't just forget me.*

I whispered, "Ed, she prayed for everyone in the family by name but me. Now she is praying for Brett, what about me?"

"She isn't finished. Give her a chance."

Before Ed finished his sentence we heard, "In Jesus name, Amen."

For our struggle is not against flesh and blood,
But against the rulers,
Against the authorities,
Against the powers of this dark world
And against the spiritual forces
Of evil in the heavenly realms.
Ephesians 6:12

"I'm out of here. This is my last vigil. First, He takes Heidi and now He will not even have someone pray for me. I hate Him." My face was red with anger and my voice was getting louder. I started to walk home.

"Lisa, where are you going? You shouldn't leave your parents," Ed called to me.

"They're fine. Pastor Vivian prayed for them. If you need me, I'll be at home. I'm done."

I overheard my parents tell Ed, "She'll be fine. Give her some time to cool down. She is under a lot of pressure – we have been waiting for this moment."

I didn't think so. I was NOT getting over this. I was beyond angry. I was hurt and I was tired of pretending everything was fine. It was not and neither was I.

I was done with the world. If they needed me; me, myself, and I would be at home sharing a whole lot of ugly with the four walls of our house.

Selfishness took over. I recognized Heidi's boyfriend was suffering but I wanted someone, especially a preacher, to realize Heidi had a sister and I was hurting too.

I left the vigil bitter and hurt, excluded and separated from my parents and sister once again. I spewed words of anger and frustration the entire way home.

Thank goodness only Ed came with me as projectile emotional vomit to God left my heart through my mouth, the entire mile back home.

I didn't want anything to do with God. I not only walked away from my family and the community that day, I turned my back and walked away from God.

Search me, O God, and know my heart;

Test me and know my anxious thoughts.

See if there is any offensive way in me,

And lead me in the way everlasting.

Psalm 139:23-24

CHAPTER 21

A time to keep...
Ecclesiastes 3:6b

A Month Later

Life seemed to be running me down. May 25, 1994, was National Missing Person's day and the same day as the first arrest in relation to Heidi's disappearance. I wanted to retreat and hide.

An escape from it all would be a blessing but fear kept me within minutes from my parents and the phone. Remember, we didn't have a cellular phone. A trip meant I would need to leave and if something happened, I would not find out until I got home. *Was my mental sanity worth the risk? Yes!*

My parents and Ed convinced me nothing would happen and if it did, we could be home in just over an hour. We still camped out on my parents' sofa sleeper so the idea of a few minutes with just the two of us sounded nice.

"Lisa, you need to get away. You can't keep living on adrenaline."

"But Mom, I won't leave you guys. What if the sheriff calls?"

"Oh Lisa, you are sleep deprived and anxious. There is *nothing* you can do. You need a break. Your father and I will be fine. We are more concerned with you right now. If you can't do this for yourself, then do it for us. We lost two daughters that day, one physically, and the other, mentally."

"I'm sorry."

"No apologies. There is no reason to be sorry. We appreciate all you do and sacrifice for us. We can't let you kill yourself trying to make us happy or care for us. We are going to be okay. One day at a time."

"Do you promise to call if anything happens?"

"Yes."

"Thank you." *Why did I need permission to leave?* One arrest in connection to Heidi's case relieved some uneasiness, so what else could happen? If Ed wanted to go, I would go.

Instead of paying off one of those debt collectors, we made hotel reservations, packed the car, and escaped. With another couple, we traveled to Toronto for a weekend. The goal, laughter and relaxation.

"Lisa, are you okay? Do you want to go back home?" My stomach was upset. Ginger ale and crackers didn't help. I wanted to tell him, "Take me back. I'm not ready." However, our marriage was

~ 164 ~

worth more than a little nausea. Mom promised to call.

"No."

"I'll turn around."

"No. We need to do this. I will be okay. I promise." *What if something happened and I was not there? Would Mom really call?*

Ed interrupted my thoughts. "Lisa, what if God is waiting for you to leave so something can happen?"

God? Please. Why bring him into this?

"Lisa?"

"I have a bad feeling in the pit of my stomach."

"Lisa, snap out of it. Your fears are holding us hostage in little ol' New Haven, New York. We can't continue to sleep in your parents' living room. There is more to life than the search center and hiding from the world." *SHUT UP. Why must he do this now? Our friends are in the back seat. Couldn't he wait until we were in our hotel room?*

I looked out the window with no response. Our friends did the same.

Do you not know?

Have you not heard?

The LORD is the everlasting God,

The Creator of the ends of the earth.

He will not grow tired or weary,

And his understanding no one can fathom.

He gives strength to the weary

And increases the power of the weak.

Even youths grow tired and weary,

And young men stumble and fall;

But those who hope in the LORD

Will renew their strength.

They will soar on wings like eagles;

They will run and not grow weary,

They will walk and not be faint.

Isaiah 40:28-32

We Arrive

In silence, we checked into the hotel. The first thing I did was call my parents. "We're here. The hotel number is…in case you need me."

"We won't. Enjoy yourselves. You deserve a break." I could almost see my mom shaking her head while saying those words with a smile on her face.

Ed and I emptied our suitcases, took a nap, and ignored each other. Anger, frustration, and a lack of patience held us captive within ourselves. The worst part was that we were not mad at each other, but at the circumstances thrust at us in our first year of marriage.

One of my aunts told us, "The first ten years of marriage are the hardest." If we made it through the first year, we would be lucky. It was going to be a long ten years. This was an understatement.

We met our friends for dinner. Their joy and excitement for the weekend was contagious. With each slice of pizza, there was less tension and more understanding. I started to remember how it felt to laugh and enjoy life. I started to believe my parents and Ed were correct. I needed this time away.

Once back at the hotel, we decided to retreat to our rooms and meet up in the morning. It was evident our friends were taking advantage of their time together, and we really should do the same. I reached for Ed's hand but pulled back before he could grasp it. His words spoken hours earlier crept back into my mind. He unlocked the door, motioning for me to go first.

Before the door closed all the way, an apology burst from my lips. "I'm sorry. I just feel guilty for leaving, for having fun, and because I left my parents."

"I'm sorry, too. I meant what I said but I never meant to hurt you. Lisa, I am worried about you. I have never seen you like this. I don't know what to do or say other than to tell you how much I love you. I am always here for you."

I fell against Ed's chest, "I'm sorry. I don't know…" He tightened his grip on me and led me to the bed. He rested my head on the pillow, dampened a washcloth with cold water and joined me. With his arms tightly wrapped around me, he held me and wiped away my tears until I fell asleep. I needed to cry. I needed to let my guard down. This was a good weekend.

In the morning, laughter and joy replaced the darkness. After a scrumptious breakfast, we traveled to Canada's Wonderland for the day. Oh my goodness, it felt good to laugh. I missed this. I missed us. I almost forgot why we were there. Our morning was full of laughter and relaxation.

After lunch, we walked around the park. I noticed the walk-around characters in front of us. I stopped so quickly that Ed ran into me. Shock froze my eyes and body. Instead of a walking zombie, I became a statue. I needed to go home.

Traumatized by Two Characters

Fred and Wilma Flintstone walked toward us. Memories flooded my brain. Heidi was such a comedian. She referred to her boyfriend, Brett, and herself as Fred and Wilma. Tee shirts, stuffed animals, and cartoons decorated her bedroom back home.

Her room was left untouched with the exception of law enforcement, and my Gram. It had been over a month. Gram cleaned her room every day so if we found Heidi, the room would be clean.

The sadness, tears, and reality returned. I should have stayed home.

"Lisa, I know what you are thinking. Let it go. Are you going to let two actors in a costume ruin a great day?" I didn't know if it was his tone or the wink and kiss to my forehead but I suppressed the tears. Instead, I returned my focus where it should have been, on my husband and our relationship.

Tired, sunburned, and exhausted, we grabbed dinner on the way back to the hotel. The original plan was to see a show in the evening but we decided to spend our evening at the hotel. We snuggled on the sofa and watched a movie. It was nearly midnight before I'd realized I had not called home all day.

"Hi Mom, just wanted to check in."

"Nothing new here, sounds like you are having fun."

"Yes. Thanks for making me come."

"It's my job. Are you still planning on going to Niagara Falls before you come home tomorrow?"

"Yes. We might even take the scenic route home. If you don't mind, that is?"

"Of course we don't mind. Enjoy yourself and be careful. Love you, good night."

For the first time in weeks, I fell asleep with a smile on my face.

Be still before the LORD
And wait patiently for him;
Do not fret when people succeed in their ways,
When they carry out their wicked schemes.
Psalm 37:7

CHAPTER 22

And a time to throw away...
Ecclesiastes 3:6b

My Worst Fear

Morning came and I felt better than I had in weeks. "Want to grab breakfast, Handsome?"

"It is nice to have you back."

"Thanks. It's good to be back."

We met our friends in the hotel banquet room for breakfast. They brought their luggage down with them so we put it in the car. After we ate, Ed told his friend, "See you in five. We have to get our stuff and check out still."

Our first silent elevator ride had been out of anger but this time it was a mutual peace. I let the weight of the world go and leaned into the man I married last year. "Thank you for a great weekend."

"It isn't over. We're going to the falls." Then he kissed me.

Ed unlocked the door and let me go in first. He went behind me to grab our suitcases but the red flashing light on the hotel room phone stopped us both.

"Ed the light is flashing. We have a message. Oh my God. Ed, what if…"

"Lisa, calm down. We do not even know who called. It might be a reminder to check out."

"Sorry, I didn't think of that. I'll call down."

I dialed the main desk in hopes Ed was right. My heart raced and my stomach muscles tightened. "Yes, this is Lisa Buske, our light is flashing. Do we have a message?"

"Yes ma'am. You need to call your mother immediately."

"What? Did she say anything else?"

"No, just to call home once you get this message."

I tossed the receiver and missed. Ed picked it up and set it down. "Lisa, what is wrong?"

"Mom called. We need to call home before we leave. We need to get downstairs. I need a pay phone."

The anxiety built. The elevator was not coming quick enough. I took the stairs. Like a team, I found a pay phone and Ed turned in our key to complete our check out, then found our friends.

"Sue called and left a message while we were at breakfast. Lisa is calling home now."

I dialed my parents' house. Someone answered. "Ken and Sue Allen's house, who is calling?"

"This is Lisa Buske. Where are my parents? What is happening? Did they find Heidi?"

The Unexpected

Once my mother was on the phone, questions flowed like the falls we would not be visiting today. "Did they find Heidi? Is she alive? We will be there as soon as we can. What do you need? Are you okay?"

Mom interrupted me. "Lisa, they have arrested another man in connection to Heidi's disappearance. You don't need to come home but we didn't want you to see it in the paper on your way home." *Of course I was coming home. How could I not?*

I dropped the phone and fell to the lobby floor, unable to speak. The receiver hung there.

"Lisa? LISA?"

"Sue, its Ed. What's up?" Ed stared at me as he listened to my mom.

"She is okay, I've got her. We will call once we are back in the United States. Yes. Thanks for calling. We're on our way."

I made Ed stop at every rest area and gas station between Toronto, Canada and New Haven, New York. The amount of money spent that morning to purchase newspapers nearly emptied our wallets. My desire to know more information overpowered me. I needed to see it with my own eyes.

"Ed, why doesn't anyone have it printed?"

"I don't know. Maybe once we cross back into New York?"

He was right. We walked into the store and there it was on the front page. More tears.

It was true. Another arrest, but where was Heidi? What about Heidi?

I clung to the news article as if it were my life force until we reached my parents' house. There were sheriff's deputies in the driveway. Dad came outside so they knew it was okay for us to be there. Would this nightmare never end?

The rest of the day was a blur. The only thing I know for sure is we did not go to the falls and there were no plans to retreat again in the near future.

We decided it was both safe, and time for us to return to our house. Some normalcy returned.

One evening Ed and I sat in the living room with the sound of Lake Ontario beating on the shore. No conversation. We enjoyed the quiet and being together, but then there was a knock at the door.

"Ed, it's my parents. Something must be wrong." My parents never stopped by without calling. My heart quickened and I remained seated.

Ed greeted them. "Hi. What's up? Is everything okay?" *I'm not ready for this, did they find Heidi?*

"We need to tell you guys something." Was it Heidi? Did they find her?

"Lisa, a local newspaper has run two cellmate statements in this evening's paper."

"Okay. Whose are they?" This was not too bad. I wasn't sure how this affected us.

"Two cellmates have given statements detailing conversations they say occurred while sharing a cell with one of the men arrested for Heidi's kidnapping and presumed death."

"What aren't you telling me? I can tell there is more. What do the statements say?"

Mom handed me the newspaper with tears in her eyes. My hand trembled as I prepared to read the words holding my parents captive. Oh my, how was it possible? Why would someone publish such detailed descriptions and horror on the front page? I didn't want to read this but knew I had to.

I tried to keep my composure as I read but the words resonated deeply.

Before the publication of these two statements, I could only imagine the torture Heidi experienced. There on the front page, in black and white were the words no mother, father, sister, brother, or child should read. *Someone doesn't make this kind of stuff up, do they?*

I read them repeatedly, hoping they would reveal something different. Unable to sit still, I decided to head to the grocery store. This would clear my mind. Well, this was the plan.

I made a mistake. I should have ordered a pizza. Customers talked about the cellmates statements as if it was some stranger and not one of their community members. While selecting produce I overheard two women talking.

"Did you read the paper? The one cell mate alludes Heidi Allen's head was smashed in with a shovel."

"I know. It is terrible. I also read her body was mutilated and burned. That is why the sheriff department confiscated a furnace."

"I don't know how the family is surviving this." *Hello? I was right there. Do you even see me? Could you be a little less inconsiderate? Was this the best thing someone could talk about in the middle of the grocery store?* I was out of there.

For a couple of weeks it didn't matter where I was, the alleged statements were the hot topic. The only places safe from the conversations were at work, my parents' house, or my Gram's. I avoided people and began to live like a hermit once again.

Time for Court

The next few months found me following the legal system through its various arraignments, motions, and personnel changes. Pre-trial motions began in May 1995 with the actual trial starting the afternoon of May 30. I wish there had been a way to still work and be at the courthouse to support my parents but reality was that the bills needed to be paid.

I went to work out of necessity with my mind focused on my parents and the trial across the Oswego River in the courthouse. Questions swirled in my brain. What was going on? Had Mom testified? Were new witnesses or information introduced? Why had no one called me to fill me in?

As soon as my shift was over, I drove faster than I should to the courthouse. They were on break when I pulled in.

"Mom, how are things going?"

"I'm glad you are here. There isn't anything new but I'm glad you're here now."

After a couple of hours in the courtroom, I followed Mom home. I was exhausted, confused, and in need of Ed.

"Ed, mom's first words to me was, 'I'm glad you are here.' It was a terrible day today. I want to be with my family."

"Lisa, take another leave of absence. We'll figure it out."

A supportive husband and employer made it possible for me to sit at my mother's side in the courtroom. Friends and family were in the courtroom, in the lobby, and outside every day for both cases.

The community continued to support us, coming with refreshments in the parking lot during the breaks. Some days my parents, aunts, uncles, and I would escape to the Press Box for lunch to avoid the cameras. It felt good to get away for lunch, out of the reach of the cameras and microphones following us in and out of the building each day.

August 7, 1995 provided some satisfaction when one of the two men arrested received a twenty-five years to life sentence for the kidnapping and presumed death of Heidi M. Allen, my beloved sister.

Tears of joy and sorrow flooded my pillow that night. Would I ever know where my sister was? I missed her. If he was guilty then why didn't he just tell us where she was? Why?

Two men arrested and tried. One guilty and the other acquitted. The discrepancy caused confusion and speculation in the community. There were two different juries and two different defense attorneys. *Would it have been different if they were tried together? Would it have worked to Heidi's favor or theirs?* We will never know.

A SIDE NOTE RELATING TO CHAPTER 22

For more information about the actual investigation or case, I invite you to visit the Oswego County Sheriff's website at http://www.co.oswego.ny.us/sheriff/allen.html.

Although Heidi has been missing for years, they continue to review her case often and investigate all new leads. Nothing is insignificant when it comes to solving a missing person's case. If you saw or remember something from April 3, 1994, I encourage you to contact the Sheriff's department. You never know if you might be holding the one piece of information to bring Heidi home. Their phone numbers are: 1-888-349-3411, 1-800-724-8477 or 315-349-3411. This is as much detail I will delve into as it pertains to the actual investigation and case. I want the focus of this book to be Heidi, not the case. Thank you for understanding.

"But as a mountain erodes and crumbles

And as a rock is moved from its place,

As water wears away stones

And torrents wash away the soil,

So you destroy man's hope.

You overpower him once for all,

And they are gone;

You change his countenance

And send them away."

Job 14:18 – 20

CHAPTER 23

A time to tear...
Ecclesiastes 3:7a

Still Missing...2006

Twelve years later, in preparation for a prayer service to remember Heidi on the anniversary of her kidnapping, the Lord spoke to me. I spent two weeks putting together my prayer. By this point I was praying daily. I hadn't taken the step to pray aloud in front of other people, though.

I searched for just the right Scripture verses and revised my prayer too many times to count. It was during this revision and writing process that I understood how foolish I had been the day I walked away from God and the vigil.

The hours, tears, and edits involved to put together a three-minute prayer exhausted me. Pastor Vivian had done this more times than I could count for Heidi and my family. Sometimes, she did them on the fly due to short notice.

I never thought of her time or the drain it must have been on her prayer life. She never complained or appeared tired, but instead she arrived with a positive attitude, ready to share God's Word, love, and her prayers with the community.

It wasn't Pastor Vivian that was in the wrong, it was me. I needed to do something to make this right...but what? Although the sun had been shining that day, my insides had been dark and destructive. I had to apologize to Pastor Vivian. Lord, could she ever forgive me?

I sat down to write her note. I apologized for my behavior, for the anger I held in my heart toward her for so many years, and for not expressing these feelings to her personally. I placed a stamp on the envelope and watched from the living room window as the mailperson removed it from the mailbox. No turning back now. It was in God's hands.

I did not have to wait long before I received a response from Pastor Vivian. Not only did she forgive me, but she also asked my forgiveness for forgetting to mention me. It wasn't intentional and she never knew how I felt. Tears instantly formed in my eyes. Why would she need forgiveness?

It was I that had been in the wrong. Forgiven. Two women at two different levels of faith, and we both learned a valuable lesson: to repent and ask forgiveness is both Biblical and healing. Pastor Vivian concluded her note by welcoming me to the family, the family of Christ.

Pastor Vivian gave selflessly of herself for years to our community and beyond. She was always there for the family as we searched, sat at the courthouse, and to this day her prayerful nature and faith in God gave her the words for each vigil she led and to forgive the hurt and lonely sister.

I know it was not intentional, and at some level, I probably always did. For over a decade, she was my scapegoat. In reality, she saved me from living a facade. I'm sure my family would have preferred a happier person on the outside, but God works from the inside out. He used Pastor Vivian to break me down – so He could build me back up.

"This is how my heavenly Father
Will treat each of you
Unless you forgive your brother
Or sister from your heart."
Matthew 18:35

Friendships of a different kind

Heidi's kidnapping affected so many people. In addition to the community and family, her friends made time to volunteer, search, and attend the vigils.

Some were from Onondaga Community College while others were schoolmates from Bishop Cunningham Jr./Sr. High School (BCHS) and Mexico Academy and Central Schools. To watch Heidi's friends spend countless hours at the center always made me smile. She was so loved, with great friends.

Prior to Heidi's kidnapping, I was the assistant coach for the BCHS girls volleyball team. This allowed me to hang out with Heidi each afternoon and attend every game, times I looked forward to and now cherish as memories. The girls worked together on and off the court, and to see them at the vigils and planning a fundraiser encouraged my entire family.

A team tradition was starting their warm-up session by doing the Hokey Pokey. In honor of Heidi, the entire volleyball team gathered at the center to do the dance. I joined in the fun. It felt good to laugh and dance. I'm thankful they still wanted me around.

One member of the team, and a dear friend of Heidi's, was Suzie, a petite, bubbly, and vibrant girl. Her energy was contagious. She dedicated hours to the center, compiling all the news clippings into a scrapbook. Her friendship and love for Heidi energized her.

As she worked, she listened for ways to be a help and encouragement. I found bookmarks, poems and little notes from her on my chair, in my car, and at my house. She always knew what I needed, when I needed it. It was as if Heidi was with me in spirit.

She completed some of the most mundane tasks with joy, saying it might be the button that brings Heidi home. Her optimism and joy were amazing. How did she do it? What gave her the strength to persevere? I desired half her energy and optimism. Even after the center closed, Suzie kept Heidi's story at the forefront.

One year behind Heidi in school, she dedicated her senior year to her friend.

"Lisa, I would like to develop a video documentary about Heidi as part of my senior project. Do you mind?"

"Of course I don't. Thank you."

"It will be a tribute to Heidi. Can I interview you and some of the family?"

"I would be honored and I am sure my family will feel the same way."

Suzie spent countless hours interviewing my parents, other family members, and me. It felt good to talk about Heidi and remember all the good times again. This project helped me more than Suzie, I think. With her project completed, Mom joined Suzie on January 10, 1995 as a guest speaker as part of the presentation for Suzie's government class.

I asked Mom, "How did it go?"

"It was emotional, difficult, and rewarding at the same time. I was able to share Heidi's story with other students preparing to enter the 'real world'. Suzie did a great job."

"I'm glad you went, Mom. I know it was hard for you but it means a lot to Suzie."

"That is why I went, for her and Heidi. She is a good friend."

"She is more than a friend, she is one good egg." We laughed at the memories.

Reflection

To remember all she did still brings tears to my eyes today. She was a blessing through this ordeal, her smile and love are imprinted on my heart.

Thank you for the joy, Suzie.

You turned my wailing into dancing.
You removed my sackcloth and clothed me with joy,
That my heart may sing to you and not be silent.
O Lord my God, I will give you thanks forever.
Psalm 30: 11 – 12

True friends are hard to come by. Suzie's positive attitude and determination exemplify friendship. God blessed me with the gift of time as I was able to get to know Suzie and the person she was and aspired to be. Suzie adopted me as her big sister. It is an honor to have her as my adopted little sister.

With her high school and college graduations complete, it was time for Suzie to be married. I remember opening the wedding invitation with a joyful smile on my face. I looked forward to watching her walk down the aisle with the love of her life.

The day of the wedding, joy and grief overcame me. Heidi would never walk down the aisle. I am thankful Suzie included me. I was blessed to watch my honorary younger sister transition from child to woman.

A Caring Community

Just as Suzie continued to remember Heidi months later, so did our community. People and businesses donated their time and materials to establish a landmark in Heidi's memory. It is a beautiful tribute. Flowers and plants that God allows to bloom each year bless the place that could be quite depressing and sad.

As part of "Make a Difference Day" in 1995, the community decided to build a star-shaped garden in the grassy lot in front of the *D & W convenience store*. Why here? This was not peaceful. It was painful. Various townspeople applied for permits, selected plants, designed the star, constructed the base, and organized a vigil to commemorate its establishment.

The original plan was to do this on Heidi's birthday but with the one-year anniversary of 9-11 only a few days before this, our precious town decided to remember Heidi and the lives lost on that fateful day. On September 15, 2002, the community gathered to remember Heidi and our nation. As the dark descended and prayers began, a domino effect of candlelight illuminated the northwestern corner of the intersection.

The candlelight and music attracted the attention of the vehicles driving by and those who stopped for gas. Some even stopped their cars to join the prayer vigil. One woman stepped out of her car. "This is a nice way to remember 9-11."

A woman's voice responded: "This isn't for 9-11, it is for Heidi Allen, a missing teenager. The family chose to do it today so we could remember our nation too, but Heidi is the first reason we are here."

It started as a small vigil for Heidi but developed into something larger than expected.

"Mom, we're out of candles."

Aunt Nancy overheard us. "I'll run home. We have some in the buffet in the dining room." I had mixed emotions as I looked around. There were so many people here to remember Heidi and our nation, and so much sadness. How would we recover...as a family and a nation? In less than ten minutes, we had enough candles for everyone.

A star built to remember one teen turned into an opportunity for people to slow down, remember and grieve. Heidi would like to know her star brought healing to those in need.

The vigil ended, yet the light remained. Instead of blowing out the candles, we placed them along the star's wooden frame. I waited until the last person left before I started for my car.

"Ed, isn't it beautiful? I am glad they built it here. We have something positive to balance out the horror of her kidnapping when we come to the store. I miss her."

"I know. You've always got me."

"Thank goodness. Can we stay a little while?"

Ed tightened his arms around me and kissed the top of my head. "Of course."

You are my lamp, O Lord.

The Lord turns darkness into light.

2 Samuel 22: 29

CHAPTER 24

A time to speak...
Ecclesiastes 3:7b

My First Public Prayer, 2006

With the twelfth anniversary of Heidi's kidnapping in a couple of weeks, I decided it was time to do things differently. I trusted God, stepped out of my comfort zone, and approached the pastor to organize a prayer service. After some discussion and prayer, the pastor agreed and encouraged me to let the Holy Spirit work in my heart.

Two weeks later, I walked into the church with my prayer typed, double-spaced in a large font, and with a friend ready to read if I was unable to finish. With God's help, I made it through the entire prayer without the need for intervention. The first of many public prayers, it was joyful to remember Heidi in prayer instead of searching the woods.

The Prayer (NOTE: Unedited to show my thoughts then, compared to now)

Dear Lord, Thank you for filling my heart with your love and giving me new strength each day as I grow in Your love, a love for myself and a love for others. Scripture says, "In Him and through faith in Him we may approach God with freedom and confidence. That is why I am suffering as I am. I am not ashamed, because I know whom I have believed, and am convinced that He is able to guard what I have entrusted to him for that day. Let us draw near to God with a sincere heart in full assurance of faith, having our hearts sprinkled to cleanse us from a guilty conscience and having our bodies washed with pure water." Ephesians 3:12, 2 Timothy 1:12, Hebrews 10:22

It is because of You and the power of the Holy Spirit that I was able to pray publicly for closure in my sister's case. A member of the church shared the importance of listening to the Holy Spirit, thank you for that message. The Holy Spirit worked through the recovery of another missing person to remind me of the importance of my praying for closure. After quiet prayer and recognizing Your answer, I was able to share this message with Pastor Rick.

Lord, thank you for the strength and wisdom to listen and follow through. You brought me to this church in 2004, and you have been doing things in me and my family ever since.

Lord, I had spent years blaming You and I could probably use the term "hating" you for what happened to my sister. I want to apologize to You and ask Your forgiveness, I apologize for my anger and the blame I placed on You for taking my sister from this earth, especially in the manner in which it occurred. I do not understand why this occurred but have since, learned many lessons because of it. The more I come to know You and Your Word, I have realized You didn't take Heidi from this earth as a punishment to her or anyone else but instead, she was chosen.

You chose her and we may never know or understand why or even understand if You decide to explain your reason, but I accept this as something You planned. I accept this now, I do not like it, but I accept it.

Dear Lord, thank You for your patience and love. In the past twelve years, hundreds, if not thousands of people have prayed for Heidi's return and/or closure in her case. Up until tonight, I have never personally asked for closure in the case. I have always hoped for Heidi's return, alive and for her to rejoin society as if she never left. I realize this is not a reality and probably always have deep within but You were patient and only gave me as much as I could handle.

Lord, I recognize that praying and asking for closure offers me more than holding on to a false hope. The past two years have been moving fast and giving me a new outlook on life. Your Psalms remind me of the direction I need to be going, "Look to the LORD and his strength. seek his face always." Psalm 105:4. The more I seek your face, the more I am reassured of Your love for me, and for everyone walking on earth.

Lord, please bring my sister home. I do not expect her to walk through the door like Tanya Nicole Kash, but I pray You bring her body home, allowing closure in her case and to the never-ending stress associated with not knowing. A wise person told me You answer prayer in one of three ways: Yes, No and Wait. I realize this is my first petition to bring Heidi home and I apologize for the years I lost with You, but I pray You answer yes. Heidi was a young, bright and energetic teenager, graduating college a year early with jobs lined up. She is the aunt of the most beautiful seven-year-old girl, with wisdom and compassion beyond her years. Closure brings hope and healing for my parents and me. Lord, I need closure. I realize You do not give more than we can handle, please continue to give me the strength to handle whatever you would choose to give me.

I love you Lord and pray You answer these prayers tonight and choose to say yes, granting closure in this case. Only You have the power to bring Heidi home, I am ready. I am ready to start to heal and live a life knowing my sister is dead, but until there is that closure, it makes the healing more difficult.

As You have said to us in Isaiah 30:19 says, "O people of Zion, who live in Jerusalem, you will weep no more. *How gracious he will be when you cry for help. As soon as he hears, he will answer you.*" *Lord I pray for closure and for Heidi's body to be found, giving her proper burial, and giving her family, friends and community the opportunity to complete the grieving process.*

Lord, Your Word tells us: "*Dear friends, if our hearts do not condemn us, we have confidence before God and receive from him anything we ask, because we obey his commands and do what pleases him. This is the confidence we have in approaching God: that if we ask anything according to his will, he hears us.*" *1 John 3:21 - 22 and 1 John 5:13*

Lord, thank You for bringing my family and friends together tonight to pray for closure. People who care and believe in Your power to answer prayer surround me. Lord God, bring Heidi home. Amen

Baptized in the Living Water

Although I chose to be baptized at the age of fifteen in the Catholic church, I did this to please my aunt and grandmother, not because I felt called by God. On June 4th, 2006, I was baptized with full immersion. I stood before God, my family, my congregation, and the three children also choosing baptism that day, as I professed my faith. My daughter was one of these children. An added blessing.

Journal Entry- June 5, 2006

Thank you God for yesterday...it was a day like no other. I believe that baptism with submersion is different and more powerful than "an outward sign of an attitude change" as stated in Matthew or by Pastor Rick. I am not saying either is wrong but the feeling is more than an outward sign, it is a great work within. Baptism, at least for me was more inward than outward.

The fear of the physical act of dunking disappeared once I plugged my nose and grabbed my right wrist. Once I closed my eyes, I heard Pastor say "I now baptize you in the name of ..." and the next thing I know is that I am standing upright and people are helping me to get out of the water. In Matthew 28:20, God said He is with me always, Amen. He was in me in a way in which I have difficulty explaining or may never be able to explain.

Wow...Amazing...Peace...Godly.

The verse in Acts 1:5 says that John baptized with the water and later God would baptize with the Holy Spirit. I believe this all occurs at the same time. It is the inner belief and prayerful heart that welcomes both the baptism of water and the baptism of the Holy Spirit. It was the words, actions and visuals over the past couple of years that have allowed God to enter into the empty spot within myself.

I have never had a faith in anyone or anything as I do in the Lord Jesus Christ. I have that today. My baptism on June 4, 2006 took away the darkness, the sin, the trouble, and the heartache and replaced it with a feeling of peace and understanding. Knowing that God loves me enough to die for me and knowing my church family was there to join me in this celebration. Wow.

Although I know it was only moments, if not seconds under the water, it felt like an eternity of peace and wonder. I was submerged in the living water of Jesus Christ... He was absorbed into me from the outside while my inward belief and love worked its way out to share with the world. As the two met, the inward love escaping to share with the world and God's living water was soaking into my pores from the outside in, the church saw water thrown from the baptismal tub. But this was not just water escaping from the tub, it was the sin, doubt, pain and lack of faith that the Lord removed from within me during my baptism. God is good...all the time and everywhere. Amen.

Revelations 22:17 says - "The Spirit and the bride say, 'Come.' And let him who heard say, 'Come.' Whoever is thirsty, let him come. and whoever wishes, let him take the free gift of the water of life." Wow...I was thirsty and I let Him come. Thank you Jesus for having so much to offer. Revelations 22 ends with "The Grace of the Lord Jesus be with God's people. Amen."

Thank you Lord for loving me so much You died for my sins, thank You for replacing a lost faith with a *newfound love, yearning and hope for the future. A stronger and deeper faith because of your love, and even stronger through my baptism in You, the living water. You are good.*

I am living proof it is possible to change when you have faith in Jesus. It is a change from the inside out. As I asked God to bring Heidi home I knew he would answer. He always answers prayer. Whether it be a yes, no, or not right now. He is faithful and does answer. I will wait.

Therefore, if anyone is in Christ,
The new creation has come:
The old has gone, the new is here!
2 Corinthians 5:17

Chapter 25
A time to mend...
Ecclesiastes 3:7a

Death versus disappearance is a topic for discussion. I have lost loved ones to cancer, a motorcycle accident, diabetes, and old age. Sadly, at least three of these were within a year of my sister's abduction.

If your brother or sister dies, as tragic as this is – at least you are able to say good-bye before they close the casket. Closure is lost when a loved one is missing because we do not know if our missing loved one is alive or dead.

In a case like my sister's, we are to "presume" she is dead, but this leaves a tiny window of hope. *Is Heidi alive somewhere? If she is, does she know how much we love and miss her?* We may never know this side of Heaven the details surrounding our missing sibling, daughter, or loved one's departure from this earth.

A Death Certificate

Due to one man's conviction for the kidnapping of my sister in the first-degree, the "presumption of death" torments my sleep and me. The next step is even worse, My parents received a death certificate for Heidi. I could have screamed – what were they thinking?

What if Heidi was still alive? She would think we have given up. Once again, I buried the frustration for the sake of my parents. I didn't understand, but knew my parents had to make choices based on legal issues beyond my understanding at that point in time.

Therefore, with a conviction and a death certificate on file, Heidi was dead to the state. However, to me, it was only a presumption. I have to keep some hope, even if it is ever so small.

Just Pray

From my parents' perspective, I can't imagine closing a casket on my precious daughter, but the thought of waking up each day to the question, "Will they find Heidi today?" causes a lump to develop in my throat. Both situations are difficult (to say the least) and invoke a gut-wrenching pain to the parent.

I am not an expert and do not believe I could say one is worse or better than the other is. I will say this: in one case, you know your child is resting with Jesus and the other, only God and the abductors know the truth. I don't understand why God allows harm to come to our children. I have heard God will bring us to our knees in order to build us up, but does He have to use a child to do this?

My Gram told me, "Parents shouldn't have to watch their children die. It is the worst pain a mother or father can face." Gram always knew how to comfort me. After she passed away, her words and inspiration remain in the depths of my memory. When my memory plays tricks on me, her journals help to fill in the blanks.

In one of her journal entries dated, June 21, 1995, she writes about my Uncle, her oldest son: "Tom passed away 7:30. Out of his suffering but don't know what more I can stand." Less than a month later, Gram wrote, "Last days...too many deaths."

While the family sat at the courthouse, we learned that tragedy struck our family again. A motorcycle accident took my cousin's life and injured her fiancé. She was nearly the same age as Heidi. Memories of my youth flooded my mind.

Missy, Shawnacy, Heidi and I were always together. Now, only Missy and I remained – our younger sisters ripped from our lives by tragedy. This was terrible. Uncle Jim was already devastated over Heidi, why God? How would we ever get through this?

On this same July day, Gram wrote, "...everyone gone to court. I'm just praying."

As the family transitioned from the courtroom to her kitchen and the hospital, she prayed. The family was distraught, to say the least, but thankfully Gram kept her heart in the right place...in prayer.

My Gram's statement, "Just pray", was how she felt. While I felt alone, Gram truly was. To fight the pain and loss, the only thing she could do was pray. In truth, prayer is the first thing we should do. Gram had it right.

A dear friend of mine does not believe we "just" pray because it is the very thing God has called us to do. We should say, "We can pray." It's a great philosophy, one I have come to treasure. It has saved me from days of despair when I feel like the world is spinning out of control around me.

Not only can we pray but we can ask others to pray for us too. We have a God who listens and is faithful to answer. Is this not a special and priceless gift? He does not always say yes, but He does answer.

This is the confidence we have in approaching God:
That if we ask anything according to his will,
He hears us. And if we know that he hears us –
Whatever we ask –
We know that we have what we asked of him.
1 John 5:14-15

CHAPTER 26

A time to be silent...
Ecclesiastes 3:7b

Priceless Moments

If you have ever lost someone to cancer you understand the slow and painful process this can be. It's difficult to watch your loved one suffer. As the observer, we experience our own pain. We want to take away their pain, but this is impossible.

In 2004, my Aunt Nancy passed away after a valiant battle with cancer. I am thankful for the time we had together both at her house and in the hospital. It was during this quiet time I was able to reminisce and say good-bye.

We laughed, cried, and prayed together. As her eyesight weakened, I read the daily newspaper to her each morning before I left for work. One night at the hospital as I watched her sleep, the tears overtook my soul. You might think they were tears for my dying aunt but they were not. They were selfish tears.

I was here to care for my aunt. I was even able to care for my Gram, but what about Heidi? I was not there for Heidi when she needed me the most. If the cellmate's statements are true, oh my gosh. She suffered a horrific death with no one there to hold her hand or help her. I wiped the sweat from my aunt's brow and covered her with another blanket. She opened her eyes to see me crying. "I'm sorry, did I wake you?"

She smiled. "No. Do not cry. I am going to be okay. I know where I am going."

"I know but I'll still miss you. I just ..."

"Lisa, in a little while, I will know where Heidi is. I'm okay."

I nodded in agreement, as one of the nurses sneaked in to set the morning paper down.

"Read to me."

"Okay." So I read.

Time in the last moments of a loved one's life is a blessing, one I experienced with most of my relatives. I didn't help Heidi. I may not like it, but I can't change it. Although I could not help my sister or hold her hand when she needed me, I know someone was with her on a spiritual level in the midst of horror. Scripture tells us the Lord is with each of us, every day and night, regardless of our location.

If I go up to the heavens, you are there;
If I make my bed in the depths,
You are there.

If I rise on the wings of the dawn,
If I settle on the far side of the sea,
Even there your hand will guide me,
Your right hand will hold me fast.
Psalm 139: 8 – 10

My Gram and Aunt Nancy modeled their trust and faith in God daily. They said good-bye to me with joy in their voices because they knew that once they closed their eyes they would spend eternity with Jesus. I am thankful for their witness in life and death. It encourages me because I will see them again one day. *Will I see my beloved sister Heidi again?* I pray yes.

"I pray that you may be active in sharing your faith,
So that you will have a full understanding of every
Good thing we have in Christ."
Philemon 1:6

Memorial or Remembrance

It is a difficult and lifelong journey to survive after you lose your sister, especially your only sister. An area I struggle with still is, "Which column do I check when I order flowers at Christmas and Easter time for the church's alter?" Do I check "in honor of" or "in memory of"?

The first ten years or so I was aggressive and rude whenever I dedicated flowers in Heidi's memory. "She is NOT dead. How dare you?" *What if this was the year we found her? You listed her with the other deceased people, how would she feel?* This was not rational thinking, but in the midst of the pain, I was not very rational.

Instead of thanking the church, family, or individual caring enough to donate toward flowers for the church in Heidi's name, I lambasted them. I admit to you right now, this was wrong and I was out of line. If I could apologize to everyone, I snapped at, ridiculed, or talked behind his or her back about his or her generosity in person, I would. Since this isn't possible, please accept my apologies here.

I was not the person I am today. I still struggle with the concept of placing Heidi's flowers with other families' deceased loved ones. It was a part of my healing. I cried for hours the first time I marked "In remembrance of Heidi M. Allen". *Please forgive me, Heidi. I love you but I need to move forward.*

God's Design

I believe Heidi's kidnapping helped me to grow into the woman God designed me to be. I would not have asked to have my sister abducted. I will venture to say that each day of not knowing has made me a stronger person.

The loss of my sister taught me to accept the trials and tribulations of life as building blocks. I allowed the blocks to weigh me down and even cover me for ten years; the best thing I did was lift each block and deal with the issue written on its side. I still lift some of these same blocks today.

I learned how precious time is through the loss of my sister. Only God knows what tomorrow brings and I do not want to take any chances. Without this life lesson, I would be a different wife, mother, daughter, friend, and sister.

I may wake up one morning without a loved one in my life anymore, but God will NEVER leave me. He is consistently there for me, waiting and watching. I pray you recognize the treasures you have in your family.

More importantly, I pray your relationship with Jesus is your most precious and cherished friendship. Thank Him today for loving and blessing you and He will bless you even more with His love.

I make a conscious choice each morning. We need to live with the mindset of change. Tomorrow or even an hour from now is not a guarantee. Do not get me wrong, I don't get up and say, "I hope no one dies today." Nevertheless, I do choose to make decisions I can live with.

You Have a Choice

The last time I saw my sister, we enjoyed a time of laughter and teasing. My calendar was marked with future sister days at the mall, doctor's appointments, and our time together. All I have now is the calendar of forfeited memories. Heidi is my sister and was my best friend. I thank God often for our closeness and friendship.

One sister shared, "My sister and I were fighting when she died; I never told her that I was sorry." God knows your hearts. You can confess your sorrow and apology to God. He will forgive you.

Sisters have a unique bond to each other; do not let one instant steal both your sister and the joyful memories you shared before the loss. Healing and forgiveness are possible.

Recognize the little things in life: to wake up, the ability to walk, to see, to hear, the food in your cupboards, the phone not ringing during your morning devotion, for your spouse doing an unexpected chore around the house, or for the rain watering the garden. Multitudes of blessings surround us every day when we slow down long enough to notice.

Too Busy to Listen

I spent years in a perpetual state of busyness. In my subconscious mind, I made sure there was no silence or down time in my schedule. I was the first to volunteer to do something for my family, friends, or at work. I never stopped long enough to be thankful or appreciative. If I was busy doing, then I did not have to think.

My idle moments were an opportunity to shout my frustration and anger to God. *Do you hear me God? How dare you take my sister? I hate you. Bring my sister back.* I demanded for God to do something, demanded if He existed that He would bring my sister home. I chuckle to think of this now.

Of course, He never answered my demands or satisfied my unrealistic and selfish requests, but I know He was there to listen and hold me when I fell into bed with nothing but tears. God listens to the cries of our heart. He hears our pain. He knows when we are discouraged. It is up to you and me to slow down and listen for His response.

Some days are easier than others are, but I long for and look forward to the quiet times now. I need them. I don't find an excuse to avoid the silence anymore. Sometimes I even schedule it on my calendar to make sure there is a designated time. I know some don't agree with penciling God in on the calendar but I believe it is the heart behind the pencil.

If you are spending time with God out of obligation, then you are not able to hear all He has for you. In my case, I schedule the time as a witness. It shows my family and God that He is worth the time.

A sister-in-Christ once told me, "Treat Jesus like you do your best friends." If you plan to meet Karen at 3:30 p.m. for coffee, are you going to write it down? Of course you are. The people who matter to us deserve our time. Jesus deserves and wants to spend time with us. If I didn't show up for coffee, Karen would be upset.

How do you think God feels when we choose to hit the snooze button or watch television instead of spending time with Him?

This helps me keep my focus. Jesus shed his blood and died for my sins, and yours. Three days later, he rose again. Jesus is my Savior, is He yours?

Blessed is the man who listens to me,

Watching daily at my doors,

Waiting at my doorway.

For whoever finds me finds life

And receives favor from the LORD.

Proverbs 8:34 - 35

CHAPTER 27

A time for war...
Ecclesiastes 3:8b

Flashback for Understanding

April 3, 1995. The first anniversary of Heidi's disappearance incarcerated me within the walls of my home. Three hundred and sixty-five days later, Heidi was still missing. I believed Heidi would be home before dinner was over that first day.

I never thought we would still be looking a year later. I chose to hide from the world rather than accept their condolences and looks of sadness.

With no intention of leaving the house, I remained in my pajamas and in bed. Ed put in an old home movie of Heidi and me. I lay in bed to cry – all day. It was the first of many anniversaries to come.

This was the routine during the first five or so years after Heidi's disappearance. Doors were locked, curtains closed, and the phone turned off. I voluntarily secluded myself from the rest of the world.

The latter part of this first decade, I started to leave the security of my home and venture out. I wanted to know where Heidi was; I was sick of waiting for someone else to find Heidi. I knew whom to call.

Veiled Truth

I picked up the phone and called a dear childhood friend. "Do you know of any psychics? I need to do something to help find Heidi."

Excited, she responded, "There is a place in Oswego. When do you want to go? It is my treat, a birthday gift."

"Name the time, I'm ready."

I missed my sister so much, I wanted her back, and I was willing to do just about anything to find her. Less than twenty minutes from my doorstep multiple business promoted occult practices.

I walked through the door of my first occult shop determined to leave with answers. The aroma of incense and drums playing in the background grabbed my attention.

The storeowner introduced herself and explained a bit about her store. She invited us to upcoming events and led me to shelves of books explaining each: angel readings, psychic readings, spirit guides, animal totems, and even a weekend event encompassing them all.

I gave the woman my money and followed her to the back. She led me into a candlelit room and the reading began. She told me everything I wanted to hear: "You've lost a loved one", "She is still missing", and "She wants you to know she is okay". Lies viewed as truth because she opened with a prayer.

"Do not turn to mediums or seek out spiritists,
For you will be defiled by them.
I am the LORD your God."
Leviticus 19:31

At first, the messages I received energized me. I ignored the uncomfortable feelings and nausea. I ignored my conscience when it said, "If you are compelled to keep it a secret, then you know it is wrong." They opened and closed each reading with a prayer. They said, "In Jesus' name..." when they petitioned for answers. Someone didn't use the name of Jesus out of context, or did they?

My family reminded me daily to "Be careful" or "You might want to reconsider this", but I di'n't listen.

Instead, I frequented the store more often and even joined my friends for a weekend disguised as a weekend of healing for women. In truth, it was an occult smorgasbord. For three days, I immersed myself in all the store had to offer.

I read books and articles. I learned how to make my own totem, to contact the angels and the other side. As we drove home, I felt so empowered, but by the time I pulled into my driveway, things changed.

Hope and excitement transitioned into regret and shame. The short drive from Von's house to my own triggered mixed emotions. Ed asked, "So how was it? Are you glad you went?"

"I'll tell you later, I don't want to scare Mary." *Oh my goodness, what was I doing?* A red flag. I probably should have reconsidered this route since I knew it was wrong to talk about it in front of my daughter. I didn't listen to the whispers in my head. I held tightly to satan's lie, blinded by false hope.

The Tenth Anniversary Of Heidi's Disappearance

April 3, 2004, the tenth anniversary of Heidi's disappearance, I took a personal day. I spent the entire day in search of Heidi based on the information obtained through years of psychic readings. With my childhood best friend by my side, we spent an entire day walking through the woods.

"Thanks for coming with me, Von."

"Anytime, I hope we find her." *Did I really want to be the person to find her?* I didn't think I could handle it. *What have I done?* I stopped and looked up.

Sometime during the afternoon, I paused and sat to listen. Birds chirped. Leaves rustled in the wind. Twigs crackled in the distance. The warmth of the sun on my face brought tears to my eyes. *Why was I crying?* "Von, do you think God cares?"

"Of course He does or we would not be here."

"I'm not sure." I returned to my thoughts.

Fast Forward to November 2004

Between the 10th anniversary of Heidi's disappearance and Thanksgiving, I continued to explore occult practices and attended a weekly message circle at a business in Sandy Creek. The psychic led this time and claimed to talk with loved ones on the other side.

She opened with prayer as usual but one night, I opened my eyes. Figuratively and literally. The room was dark and spooky. *If we are talking to God, shouldn't the room be full of light and hope? Why was it so dark?*

There was a tugging on my heart. An indescribable feeling but it was different from anything I'd felt before. It wasn't an "it", I think it was a "who" tugging on my heart – but who was it? The circle concluded and I was ready to leave.

Once the lights were on, the storeowner started to tell all of us about a Christian church in the area. They were praying, protesting, and working to have her business close. *What? If this was of God, and you had a relationship with God, then why would a Christian church run you out of town?* Something is askew. "Excuse me, but if we're praying to Jesus, then why are they doing this?"

Someone across the room replied. "They don't believe in using spirit guides and ghosts, even though they are in the Bible."

"Is it really wrong...I mean, against the Bible?"

No one answered my question but continued his or her tirade toward the church. I didn't return for another message circle after that. I was lost and hopeless again. I couldn't and wouldn't trust God. The only thing I put my faith in was a lie and bad for me. What would I do now?

Regardless of the number of readings or message circles I participated in, the emptiness remained. The void was replaced temporarily with a false hope. Due to the lies, darkness and despair returned shortly after I returned home each time. The thoughts that encouraged me during the day haunted me during the night. It was time to walk away and not look back; there had to be something better.

God is Faithful

Unable to find anything or anyone to fill the void I decided to return to college and complete my college degree. I started with my associate's degree and my New York State Teacher's Assistant certification. During this process, I was determined to be the best person I could be, using education as the band-aid for the grief and loss.

One evening I joined my friends from work for dinner at Admiral Woolsey's in Oswego. The evening was going well and then something snapped. I don't remember the details that triggered the yelling but I remember the outcome and the honest help of a friend. As with most intense moments, we retreated to the ladies' room for privacy.

The fireworks started riverside and the healing began inside, literally. Beth held me square in front of her, a hand on each of my shoulders, "Lisa, you need help. If you will not talk to me, then find someone else. I love you and don't know what to do to help you." *I've heard this before.*

"What do you want me to do? I don't know how I feel. I don't know what you want me to say?"

No more words.

Nothing but tears.

Continuous, hard, and from the heart.

Would anything take away the pain? Would anything bring my sister back? Would I ever feel whole again?

I don't suggest using the occult, education, or work to fill your void. It was a difficult and painful journey. I do not condone my behavior and will not make excuses, but I know without these pieces, I would not be the person I am today.

Most importantly, without my education and teacher's assistant certification, I would not have met the young man God used to transform my life.

In December of 2002, I accepted a position as a teacher's aide for the Mexico Academy Central Schools and advanced to teacher's assistant in September of 2003. The opportunity to work with the same class for the first three years of my employment proved to be a blessing.

A career didn't change me, the children and the friendships with the teachers did. God used the students and my colleagues at New Haven Elementary to open my heart to grieve, heal, and invite Jesus in to my life.

He said to them,

"Do you bring in a lamp to put it under a bowl or a bed?

Instead, don't you put it on its stand?

For whatever is hidden is meant to be disclosed,

And whatever is concealed

Is meant to be brought out into the open.

If anyone has ears to hear, let them hear."

Mark 4:21-23

CHAPTER 28

A time for peace...
Ecclesiastes 3:8b

A Child Leads Me

One student in particular has a special place in my heart. Jonathan is quiet, enjoys reading a good book whenever he can, and loves a challenge. I wonder if this is why we got along so well. I was a big challenge so God used a child. He knew the way to my heart.

I had the opportunity to work in a small group with him and another student on a research project. Their energy and desire to learn excited me and I found myself working into the wee hours of the night for a new tidbit they could devour.

I can still hear Jonathan: "Mrs. Buske, make sure you go to bed tonight. Don't stay up too late. You need your rest."

With a smile, I always assured him, "Of course. I'll do my best."

One day he surprised me with his wisdom. "Why are you always so busy?"

I was honest with him. "I don't know, Jonathan." A look of sadness came over his face. "I'll think about it and let you know tomorrow. Okay?"

"Yes."

The following morning I heard, "Good morning, Mrs. Buske. Did you figure out why you are so busy?" *Why is this such a difficult question to answer? I honestly did not know but I hoped he believed me.*

"I don't know."

Without blinking an eye he said, "I know."

I looked at him with wonder and curiosity. I leaned down to hear his thoughts, expecting a philosophical explanation. "I hope *you* didn't stay up all night thinking?" I said with a chuckle.

He was not laughing. "Mrs. Buske, do you go to church?"

I could tell this was important to him. I couldn't lie to him but I didn't want to tell him the truth either. He was a pastor's kid. I answered, "Not in a long time."

"Will you come to my church on Sunday?" *Oh no God, you won't trick me into going to church. How would I tell Jonathan no when his heart was so heavy and honest? I had to go, but only once.*

"Maybe, I…"

"Mrs. Buske, you need Jesus. Please." *Oh my gosh, how do I get out of this conversation?*

"For you Jonathan, yes." *Did I just say that?*

"Promise?"

"I promise. What time does church start?"

"You can call my Dad." Now I had to talk to the pastor. Thank goodness, I liked this kid.

Once home, I told Ed. He encouraged me to go, but he wouldn't come with me. I called the pastor to find out when the service started and added it to my calendar. I only had to go once to keep my promise. *You win this one God, one Sunday.*

Did I mention this was the Sunday following Thanksgiving? It was. I made the short drive and entered the church. After some conversation with the pastor, I decided to attend Sunday school prior to the service. This way if it was bizarre or weird, I could leave. I will have kept my promise without staying for the service. This was a good plan until God started to work in my heart.

Once through the door I scanned the room for an open seat. Before I could take another step, I was welcomed with handshakes, introductions and multiple invitations to "sit with me". I didn't see Jonathan. The Sunday school offered three classes so everyone could learn at their level. The adults met in the sanctuary, the teens at the parsonage, and the children in the front.

I would have to wait until Jonathan sees me after Sunday school before I could leave. These thoughts quickly left my mind. I might be meeting each of these people for the first time but they extended more love to me than I felt in years. I wanted to cry. No tears fell. The wall was too thick.

After Sunday school, I waited to see Jonathan. He saw me and smiled. I smiled back as I fought back tears. "A promise is a promise. Thank you." He did not respond. He only smiled.

I am forever grateful for the invitation extended by a child. He led me to more than a church. He brought me to Jesus. I learned how to love Jesus and the importance of having a relationship with Him.

I walked out the door of the Community Alliance Church in New Haven, overwhelmed and hopeful. Although the drive home was only a few minutes, it took me nearly a half hour because I had to drive around the country block until I could stop crying. *Why was I crying?* This was amazing. I forgot how it felt to have hope.

I don't remember the exact Sunday I accepted Christ in my heart, but I will never forget the young man God used to tell me, "Mrs. Buske, you need Jesus." He was so right.

> *He reached down from on high and took hold of me.*
> *He drew me out of deep waters.*
> *He rescued me from my powerful enemy,*
> *From my foes, who were too strong for me.*
> *They confronted me in the day of my disaster,*
> *But the Lord was my support.*
> *He brought me out into a spacious place.*
> *He rescued me because he delighted in me.*
> Psalms 18:16 – 19

I found the "what" and "who" I spent years looking for. I have not been the same since that Sunday morning. God knows our innermost thoughts, needs, and weaknesses. I encourage you to trust the Lord and recognize the little things he places in your path.

It might be a child with the strength, courage, and boldness to tell you what you need. Nothing will take the place of my sister, but God will hold me in the shadow of His wings while I wait.

Sisters-In-Christ

Reflecting on the days following Heidi's kidnapping I remember the words of encouragement shared by one of my sister-in-laws. She said, "Don't worry, Lisa. You still have four sisters left and we love you."

I would like to tell you I responded in love but I did not. Anger and hurt spewed from my mouth, "You are NOT my sisters and never will be."

I have apologized to my sisters-in-law since this day and asked their forgiveness but at the time, this was how I felt. I didn't want someone to claim my sister's relationship. I wanted her and no one else. My parents told me, "Never say never". God showed me it is possible to love and cherish sisterhood once again.

In 2006, a women's Bible study taught me to appreciate the value of sisterhood. Once a week I joined the other women in the church for a Bible study. I was hungry to learn how the Scripture applied to my life today. Only one part of this group bothered me, the closing.

The leaders encouraged us to share personal praises and prayer requests. This aspect of the Bible study made me anxious but I learned to appreciate and look forward to it in a short time. I found it is during this very intimate time of prayer that we are able to truly see another's heart.

Prayers spoken and answered. This time of sharing our deepest concerns with each other taught me to trust again and cherish the friendships birthed during this time.

Once a week, on Thursday, Heidi and I got together for "sister day". Regardless of our schedules, we kept Thursday open for each other. Sometimes it involved a trip to the mall while others were spent sitting around the house to watch a movie. We remembered days of the past with dreams of our children playing together. "Sister Day" was ours and we looked forward to being friends as adults too.

I have come to look forward to the time spent with the women at church. The Bible study, praises, prayers, and lessons help to fill my spiritual needs at a deeper level. In addition to meeting my spiritual needs, the void left from the loss of "sister day" is restored through the relationship with my girlfriends, and even some of Heidi's friends.

More Than One

I may have lost my birth sister in 1994 but years later, I have not one sister but many. Sisters are important for a woman's survival. I went from one sister, to four sisters-in-law and a multitude of sisters in God's family.

But I call to God, and the Lord saves me.

Evening, morning and noon I cry out in

Distress and he hears my voice.

Psalm 55: 16 –17

CHAPTER 29

What does the worker gain from his toil?
Ecclesiastes 3:9

Patience, faith, and a positive outlook does not come easily. There is work involved. From 1994 to 2004, I put my trust in law enforcement, my parents, neighbors, friends, family, and psychics.

While my trust wasn't in God during these times, He planted seeds of hope and love in my life, some as simple as a note in the mail said, "I'm praying for you" to the birth of our daughter.

As I look back over the darkest years in my life, I see examples of God's love and provision. He brought people into my life to make this journey easier to bear.

Around 2001, Doug and Mary Lyall from the *Center for Hope* in Ballston Spa, New York contacted my parents. Their daughter Suzanne Lyall, who was kidnapped on March 2, 1998, remains missing. They wanted to make sure my parents knew about the *New York State Missing Person's Day* on April 6th, 2001 in remembrance of Suzanne's birthday and for all the missing persons in our state.

Mr. Lyall invited my parents and the entire family to the state capital, Albany, to participate in this event. My parents were encouraged and touched by the invitation but were not ready to attend something like this.

Mom called me. "Lisa, there will be a day of remembrance in Albany on April 6th. Your father and I don't plan to attend but if you would like to, you can. It is open to the entire family."

"I'll go if someone goes with me."

"You call Missy and I'll call Jim, Martha and Nancy."

Invited to Albany

It was unanimous. We would attend. Mr. Lyall requested newspaper clippings, photographs of Heidi, and extra missing person fliers for a display. It was exciting to be doing something to bring Heidi's name back to the forefront. With the necessary information sent out, it was time to organize who was going and how we would travel there.

Aunt Nancy, Uncle Jim, Auntie M, Missy and I started for Albany early in the morning. While the ride was a little over three hours, it passed quickly with all the conversation and laughter. It had been awhile since we traveled together, especially one with so much happiness.

With only one missed turn, a handful of fliers, and a parking space secured – we made our way to the correct building. Albany was quiet on a Sunday so we only needed to concentrate on the signs and security guards leading the way to our destination.

Once off the elevator we followed the sound of voices down the hall. It was a jovial group of people. How were they able to be so happy? I wasn't sure I was ready for this. I should have stayed home with my mom. A woman bearing one of the biggest smiles I have seen came toward us.

"Hi, you must be Lisa. My name is Mary Lyall. We are so glad you all could make it. Follow me." An amazing strength was wrapped up in this woman. She and my mother would get along great.

"Yes, hello, Mrs. Lyall."

"Call me Mary, please."

I introduced her to my aunts, uncle, and cousin. With the formalities out of the way, she led us into the meeting room. It was beautiful. *Why did my heart ache so badly?* There was a beautiful bouquet of yellow roses as the focal point with handmade flowers in a vase to the side. Each one had one of New York's missing on it. Tears welled in my eyes as I realized, Heidi is one of the flowers. She was one of so many I never knew existed.

"Mary, are each of these people still missing?"

"Yes, and there are so many more. So many more."

Mary excused herself to return to her role as coordinator and greeter. Missy and I headed in one direction with our aunts and uncles going in the other. Uncle Jim was already talking politics and investigation details with someone.

Our aunts found a place for us to sit before they started to visit with those around them. There were tables along two of the walls with fliers, buttons, and other items to display each of the remembered missing persons of the day.

Up until this day, I had not met another family who lost a loved one to abduction or kidnapping. During the service, each family had the privilege to place the flower depicting their loved one in the vase of yellow roses. My family let me place Heidi's flower, a moment to remember our missing loved one.

As I walked to the front, I saw Heidi's photograph on the screen with her birth and missing dates listed. I realized other families understood the loss and heartache I carried in my heart, the room was full of them. There was healing. The concourse of the capital building would house the floral arrangement on Monday morning as a tribute to our missing.

There were words of encouragement, political thanks, a video remembrance and music. Brittany Kissinger sang "Whispers", a song written by her brother for their friend, Suzanne. His words, her voice, and their love for a friend invoked a room full of tears.

"Missy, I saw her CD's out on the table. We need to buy one before we leave. My mom needs to hear this song." Missy agreed.

Another Sister

A private reception for the families concluded our time together. At first, I was quiet; there was so much to take in. I was not sure what to say or do. *Why was this so difficult? Wasn't everyone here in the same situation as we were, looking for his or her loved one?* As I walked to the back of the room, I noticed a woman close to my age so I introduced myself.

"Hi, my name is Lisa."

"Hi, my name is Sandy."

I regret to tell you I don't remember all the details of this conversation. I know we talked quite a bit. As we shared our personal stories, our sisters' names, ages, and the details of their kidnappings, healing started to take place. Sandy and I had a lot in common, both at a personal level and with our sisters' cases.

She was the first person I talked to in eight years who understood, without words, how I felt. She was also the sister left behind to find her role in the family again. We shared our hearts, hopes and fears, a bond only a sister understands.

There was one major difference. Sandy still had her faith in God. *How? Why?* She has lost her sister but has a sense of peace about her, and maintains hope for the future. I struggled to understand this but craved it at the same time.

For the Spirit God gave us does not make us timid,
But gives us power, love and self-discipline.
2 Timothy 1:7

Absorbed into our own conversation, we failed to notice the time. Missy snapped us back to the present. "Sorry to interrupt, but Dad and everyone want to head out. We have a long drive ahead of us."

"Okay. Missy, this is Sandy."

"Hi, nice to meet you...Lisa, I'll let them know you are coming."

"Thanks."

Sandy and I said good-bye and looked forward to the next time we would meet. I finally met another sister, someone that understood and could relate, and I had to leave. It would be another year before I saw her. I was both discouraged and encouraged. I joined my family for the trip home.

The Next Step

The *Center for Hope* invited my cousin Missy and me to join their team in Ballston Spa for a smaller gathering to brainstorm for future missing person days. Our husbands watched our children so we could make this venture together. It was good to see Sandy again and to meet different families in a much more informal level than our trip to Albany.

Throughout the weekend, families shared their loved ones' cases, memories, and stories. A statement we heard often was, "You are lucky to have the level of support you do with your law enforcement agency."

I have always believed in our Oswego County Sheriff's Department but to hear some of the neglect, harassment, and poor investigation across the state in other cases – I am even more appreciative. Mom and Dad needed to know how blessed we were too.

I honestly don't recall exact details for the business portion of the weekend. There were guest speakers, family members, and a lot of information shared.

I was overwhelmed to say the least, while Missy absorbed it all. I think one of the most important things that happened during this trip was the friendship and bond restored between my cousin Missy and I.

In the afternoon we visited the little shops along the main street and in the evening, we relaxed and got to know each other again. Our room was full of laughter, tears, and a comfortable silence.

"Thanks for coming with me, Missy. We both lost our little sisters. Thank goodness we have each other."

"I will always be here for you. All you have to do is ask."

Since the first *New York State Missing Person's Day*, both it and I have grown. Instead of a small meeting room in the capital building, the *New York State Museum* opens its doors and hearts for the *Center for Hope* to host this annual event. Evidence people care about the missing.

I always enjoy the time with my Uncle Jim and Cousin Missy as we make this trek. At first, it was a "need" to have them with me, now it is a desire and joy.

Doug and Mary Lyall's mission from new legislation to the *New York State Rememorial* are only the beginning. They continue to help locate the missing and provide support for their families within New York's boundaries and beyond.

National Support

Kidnapped at the age of eighteen, legally an adult but still a child. Heidi worked full-time to put herself through college. In 1994, the *National Center for Missing and Exploited Children* (NCMEC) was unable to help us because of her age.

Thanks to the Lyalls' dedication and President George W. Bush's signature in 2003 on Suzanne's Law, Heidi is now included in the National Crime Information Center (NCIC) and the NCMEC database. Law enforcement must notify NCIC when someone between the ages of 18 and 21 is missing.

At the time of Heidi's disappearance, I was disappointed because NCMEC couldn't help us. I was disappointed, discouraged, and unable to do anything to make a change. I don't even know where I would begin. Thankfully the Lyalls did.

NCMEC assigned a case manager to the family immediately, even though it was years since her disappearance. Cases like Heidi's offer age-progression fliers too. Each flyer distribution triggers a mailing to my parents so we know the new areas receiving a flyer with Heidi's information and photographs on them.

This blessing saves the family time and money. NCMEC has the potential to reach locations the family wouldn't have access to without their support. While this is vital in the recovery of missing children, NCMEC is so much more than a poster distribution agency.

Another way they help the family is with moral and emotional support through one of their extensions, *Team Hope*. *Team Hope* is an arm of NCMEC designed to offer peer support to a family after their loved one goes missing.

Team Hope consists of mostly volunteers, mothers, fathers, brothers, sisters and other relatives of missing or exploited children. In less than twenty-four hours from Heidi's entry into the NCMEC database, my parents received a phone call.

NCMEC also partners with schools, businesses, and organizations to raise awareness for child safety through the *Ride for Missing Children*. *The Ride for Missing Children* (RMC) started in 1995 when seven men rode their bicycles from Utica, New York to Washington, D.C. to raise awareness for the plight of missing children, arriving on May 25th – National Missing Children's Day.

Two years later, with 43 riders and the same mission, they rode from Albany, New York to Utica, New York. As of today there are five rides held across New York State each year with hundreds of cyclists at each ride.

The dedication of the riders, volunteers, and law enforcement is an inspiration, especially to the family's of the missing and exploited children.

CHAPTER 30

I have seen the burden God has laid on men.
Ecclesiastes 3:10

One Child at a Time

I attended my first ride in 2008. My cousin Missy went the previous year. She came home excited and encouraged me to join her the following year. At first, I was hesitant, but I agreed to go. I didn't understand why someone who doesn't have someone missing would ride a bicycle one hundred miles. It did not make sense to me.

Although the actual ride was on Friday, the family gathered from Thursday to Saturday. Thursday evenings were a quiet time for the families of the missing to meet and lean on each other for support. I had the opportunity to meet other siblings and parents searching for their loved ones. As soon as I entered the room, I was with family.

"Hey, Missy. Thanks for the encouragement to join you. This is amazing."

"Wait until tomorrow morning."

"You mean it gets better?"

"To say the least."

Before the sun rose on Friday morning, we boarded a bus to join the riders before they started their ride. There were nearly four hundred riders at the first *Ride for Missing Children* (RMC) I attended. Most used personal or vacation time in order to ride their bicycles for one hundred miles "To keep our children safer, one child at a time." This is the theme of the ride. Some riders also spend time at the local schools in the weeks leading up to the ride to meet the students and share safety rules with them.

Family members of missing children share their loved one's story as part of the opening ceremony on Friday morning as a reminder of the reason they are pedaling their bicycles. It was more than a bike ride, it was a mission.

As the riders mounted their bicycles, we gathered at the entrance to encourage them for the day's ride with "Amazing Grace" on the bagpipes in the background.

The families loaded onto the "family van" the moment the last bicycle exited the drive. Once loaded, we joined the procession of nearly four hundred riders. Throughout the day we alternated between following behind the riders, bypassing them so we could cheer them up the big hills, and join them at the schools to hand out pencils and stickers to the students. It was a long day.

I was exhausted without pedaling a bike; how did they do it? I wondered if they knew how much we appreciated all they do. Thank you didn't seem like enough. They were an inspiration to the family members still searching and those with answers.

A Larger Family

One hundred miles of sweat, tears, and pulled muscles ended with one final ceremony that evening. I started the day with riders and the families of other missing children but when I boarded the bus to return to the hotel – I was part of a new family, the RMC family. People united to keep our kids safe and remember the children lost and exploited.

My goal is to attend at least one ride a year. These people are amazing and need to know how much we, the families, appreciate and value them in our lives. With each pedal of their bicycle, hope spins its beauty for the community to see.

Ride for Heidi

An aspect of the *Ride for Missing Children,* unfamiliar to many, is their summer ride. Each year, the RMC – Mohawk Valley holds a special ride. While those watching them ride in their matching jerseys will remember all missing children, the riders ride for one child and his or her family in particular during this ride.

The summer ride in July 2008 was in remembrance of my sister, Heidi Allen. Our daughter, Mary, and I experienced the ride before, but this was my parents' first experience. One rider was unable to attend so she sent me a beautiful angel figurine. It's a precious gift that reminds me each day of God's provision through NCMEC and the ride.

With their pink, turquoise, purple, and black jerseys on, they rode their bicycles over fifty miles to let my parents, and the entire family know Heidi would not be forgotten. My daughter yelled, "Here they come!" as she ran to join us at the driveway's edge.

Two by two with a Sheriff's escort, they rode through my parents' circular driveway. My parents, Ed, Mary, Sheriff Todd, extended family, and neighbors encouraged the riders – "Thank you.", "Keep up the good work", "Beautiful", and even a, "God bless you".

The riders' response: "No, thank you." or "We will never forget Heidi", as they wiped tears from their eyes. I wonder if they knew what a blessing they were to my family and me. Thank you didn't seem like enough. I didn't know what else I could say.

Two riders at the end of the procession stopped and dismounted their bikes to introduce themselves to my parents. My parents smiled and wiped tears from their eyes. Before I knew what was happening, my parents excused themselves with an invitation for these two amazing men to join them inside the house.

I watched as they walked into my parent's house, for a private conversation. May God bless Dick and Frank, they have two of the biggest hearts for our missing children and the families left behind.

As the other riders made their way past D & W and the *Heidi Allen Community Garden* – a private conversation restored hope in my parents' hearts. Dick and Frank mounted their bicycles to rejoin the riders while we scurried to our cars so we too could join them for lunch.

Our church put together a luncheon for the riders so they wouldn't have to travel with bag lunches in the heat. It was a beautiful sight to see the bikes scattered about the churchyard with riders stretching in the grass, visiting with our church family, and replenishing their water supply.

Once the last two riders arrived, it was time for lunch. Pastor Sheets opened our time together with prayer before the buffet line opened. The riders had only been there a few minutes but the laughter and conversation sounded more like a family reunion, not a first time meeting.

A hanging plant was not enough to say thank you, but it was, because no one there expected anything in return for what he or she did. There was still good in the world.

A woman from church stood with me. "I understand why you enjoy going to the rides so much now. They are wonderful."

"Yeah, to say the least."

"Lisa, thank you for letting us be a part of this day with you." I nod and smile, then tears.

"Thank you for putting together lunch, it is delicious and they appreciate it more than you know." I thought there was a surplus of food but after the riders were finished, little left overs remained. There's never enough starch on ride day. *Was there a way to talk with each rider personally?* Hmm...I didn't want them to leave.

With lunch complete, the riders returned to their bicycles to make their ride back to Camden.

"Ed, can we follow them until they reach Parish?"

"Of course. Grab Mary and we'll go."

With the sunroof open, we raced to the car. Mary was bubbling with excitement. "This is great. Can I stand in the sunroof?"

As we passed the riders, Mary's wish came true as she stood to cheer the riders on. "Thank you. You're doing great." Such joy in her, she truly looked up to each one of the riders. I wonder if they realized the role model they became for her.

It Starts with One

One year at the Albany ride, my daughter, nine or ten years of age at the time, spoke at the closing ceremonies. Her words spoke volumes and were more mature than her years.

"You have motivated me. When I get home, I am going to learn how to ride my bike so I can ride alongside all of you one day, until there are no more children missing. Thank you for riding for my aunt and all the missing children."

These may not have been her exact words but it is the best summary I can share with you.

The purpose of the ride for missing children is keeping our children safe and to raise awareness. The ride helps to raise monies for missing person fliers to be printed and to do safety presentations within the schools.

As I listen to my daughter speak at RMC events, it warms my heart to see their goal unfold in front of them. Before my daughter attended her first ride, she would second guess herself and say, "What can I do? I am only a kid."

I believe children are one of the strongest and most influential assets we have in our communities. It took one child to share Jesus with me, which thereby led me to share Jesus with my family and all of you reading this book.

I encourage my daughter daily to be the best she can be, to trust God, and lean not on her own understanding. (Prov. 3:5) As she watches the riders' dedication and love for missing and exploited children, she always cries.

Each time she watches the riders interact with the students at the school stops she smiles and says, "I want to be like them when I grow up, Mom. Kids need good role models."

To some the RMC is one day a year, but to the families of missing and exploited children, it is a constant reminder there are people who will never forget our missing loved ones. As long as the RMC continues, there is hope.

Children are safer because of the education and discipline exhibited with each cyclist. Missing children are recovered because of posters printed by NCMEC with the proceeds of the RMC. I may not ride a bicycle alongside them but I do pray as they train, teach, and ride.

Organizations like the *Center for Hope, The National Center for Missing and Exploited Children, Team Hope, The Ride for Missing Children,* and *The Surviving Parent's Coalition* each strive to empower the victim and their family to survive.

My life is better because of the people I have met through each of these organizations. They are an inspiration. They do not let tragedy keep them down but insteaduse it as the fuel for their priorities in life.

Their energy, heart, and compassion are contagious. It is an honor and blessing to know each one and call them not my friends, but an extension of our family. They are a constant reminder – it is possible to survive tragedy.

No Longer Silent

My involvement with NCMEC has empowered and motivated me to help others, especially the siblings left behind after a kidnapping. I was blessed at the first ride I attended. I spent most of the day as an observer, overwhelmed by the outpouring of love and support from the community.

Since then I have added the role of speaker to my involvement, sharing Heidi's story and the impact of the ride on my life as part of the day's events. I even had the honor to write a column in the monthly newsletter to share other families' stories and their thoughts about the RMC.

If someone suggested I speak and write about my story in 1994, I would have laughed it off. But today, I look forward to the people I will meet and pray to be the best writer, speaker and person I can be – sharing hope with other siblings and those affected by kidnapping.

The LORD your God is with you,
The Mighty Warrior who saves.
He will take great delight in you;
In his love he will no longer rebuke you,
But will rejoice over you with singing.
Zephaniah 3:17

Chapter 31

He has made everything
Beautiful in its time.
He has also set eternity
In the hearts of men;
Yet they cannot fathom
What God has done
From beginning to end.
Ecclesiastes 3:11

This may be the last chapter of the book, but in truth, it is more of a beginning. I spent years in prayer about this very chapter. After all, Heidi is still missing, so how can I close the book?

In a sense, there is some closure with one man serving a twenty-five years to life sentence for her kidnapping and presumed death, BUT she has not been recovered, so her case and the search are still open.

My realization...life will never be the same, even if the case is solved and marked closed. Heidi may be missing but she is not forgotten. This book might end, but my desire to help others has only just started.

In 2006, I wrote the first draft as part of the 3-Day Novel Writing Contest out of Canada. I sent in my registration and fifty dollars. I never expected to win, but I used the contest as a way to release the emotions and thoughts consuming me. In essence, the first draft was nothing more than my "emotional vomit" accumulated over twelve years.

In a handwritten note, one of the judges encouraged me to finish my book because people needed to hear my story. At that point in my life, I had no desire to share my story, I just needed to get it out. With no desire to revise, edit, or add to this vomit, I put it on the shelf for a couple of years.

In 2008, the development and revision began to transform the "emotional vomit" into a story others might want to read. The mental exhaustion weighed me down and was more than I could bear, so it returned to the shelf where it would collect more dust.

Called to Write

Without any warning, in 2010, my inspiration to write returned. Each Spring I enjoy the *Alliance Women's Refresh* retreat weekend with the women from my church. I always return home refreshed and motivated but this year in particular, a flyer at the registration table peaked my interest. A sense of peace and inspiration stirred within, it was time to finish my book.

In less than three months, the *Upstate New York Christian Writer's Gathering* at the *Delta Lake Bible Conference Center* offered an opportunity to explore my interest and desire to write for Him. As soon as I saw the flyer, my heart soared and my dust-covered manuscript came to mind.

I called home and told my husband, "There is a writer's conference in July, can I go?"

"If you want to, why are you asking me?"

"I don't know, but I believe God is calling me to Delta Lake for this conference."

"Then go." And so began my excitement and desire to write for God.

My first real venture alone since Heidi's kidnapping was to attend the writer's conference. A trip I made by myself. At first I was nervous about the drive or if I was ready to finish the book. As soon as I stepped out of my van, I could feel God's arms wrapped around me as if to say, "You are okay. I'm right here." *I was supposed to be here, Lord lead and protect me.*

I heard God speak to me in ways I never experienced before. I called home the first night. "Ed, God wants me to finish my book, and now."

"I know. We all know. we were just waiting for you to be ready."

"What? You're not surprised."

"No, I would only be surprised if you came home not wanting to finish." I spent a good portion of my evenings in tears. Overwhelmed at how God provided for me, for the support I had in my husband, and for a family who believed in me.

"I can write this book and I will."

Through the presenters, I learned ways to improve my craft, to establish my platform and how to market myself. I called my daughter. "Do you know how to develop a website? What is a blog? Is that something you can help me with?"

"Yes, Mom. I will start now. When will you be home?"

While I made the one-hour drive home, my daughter spent time on the Internet. Before Ed could open the door, she was there. "Mom, I found three. Come on."

My husband smiled and motioned me to join them at the computer. "She has been working since she hung up the phone. I am proud of you. Go. I'll bring everything in."

In less than twenty-four hours, I had a functional website and blog. I reviewed my notes and handouts and made a list. *I love lists.* So much to do before I even started to seek publication. *This is in*

Your hands, God. Be with me. I spent the next year investing time, energy, and prayer to establish my writing ministry.

More than Writing

Each morning and evening during the writer's gathering, I attended worship services and Bible teachings. I learned to be a better writer as I trusted God for the strength and wisdom to move forward. It felt as if the speakers planned their message just for my heart. *How did they know what I needed to hear?*

Of course, they had no idea, but God did. He is faithful. Uplifted in the knowledge God was with me, I set out to write. But where and how would I start? Could I implement all I have learned? God answered before I left the tabernacle area.

One evening on my way back to my room, a woman approached to introduce herself. "Hi, my name is Elaine. Are you here for the writing conference?"

"Yes, my name is Lisa."

"God told me to come over and introduce myself to you." *Me? Why?*

"Oh." *Did I run or stay?* I had better stay. God always has a plan.

"What are you writing?" *What, Oh my goodness, I had to say it aloud. Lord, I don't know if I can, give me the strength.*

"My sister was kidnapped in 1994 and is still missing. I've written a book to help other siblings." I fought back tears.

"Oh my goodness. You need to write this story. Are you here for the entire weekend? "

"Yes."

I don't remember the rest of the conversation. It faded into the darkness but Elaine's faith, obedience, and compassion encouraged me. I looked forward to seeing her the next day. We smiled at each other but didn't have much in the way of conversation.

God planted the seed of friendship that night. During the next year, Elaine mentored and encouraged me to finish. At the 2011 gathering, we were friends, reunited with many stories to share. Her friendship and mentoring continue to be a blessing in my life.

Where Do I Start

I was home and ready to finish the rewrite and revisions, but I struggled to implement an organized manner to do this. Once again, God met this need. At the first gathering, one of the speakers could not attend so the *Wit & Wisdom* writer's group did a presentation. They lived close to me and I wondered if they had room for one more member.

I didn't think to share my contact information at the conference. God orchestrated our meeting in spite of my forgetfulness. They invited me to join them one morning and review my first chapter. I was nervous and excited. I knew they were all busy working on their own writing projects.

Why were they helping me? I joined them around the kitchen table as they introduced themselves again. They provided valuable feedback and guidance so I could move forward, and finish the book.

With their help and critique, I started to rewrite, revise, and add to my original draft. Although they were not expanding their writer's group, they took time to help me get started. I added their suggestions to the multitude of lessons learned at the conference and went to work. I emailed my first revision to them for another critique. It was wonderful. I learned so much from their thoughtful and challenging comments.

God never left me when Heidi was kidnapped. I left him – a message I hope you heard throughout this book. God provided a network of writers to help me through the metamorphosis of wannabe-writer to Christian author.

The Lord gifted me with the ability to write and express myself. A small audience of my mom, sister-in-law and a few friends spurred me to be the writer I am today. Only God could have seen this coming.

Retreat and Write

At the 2011 *Upstate New York Christian Writers' Gathering,* God guided my pen to write this chapter. The Holy Spirit nudged me, opened my ears and ministered to my heart.

As I sat on a makeshift bench with Delta Lake's sparkling water below me, a woodpecker tapped in beat with each ripple as it hit the rocky shore, and a dear friend was on the swing behind me – the words flowed. Tears of healing, hope, confirmation, and completion trickled down to blot the paper.

The writing of this book ends where it began, at the *Delta Lake Bible Conference Center,* but the end of the book is the beginning of a new Lisa. I am a different person because of the trials and tribulations these past few years.

Heidi may still be missing but her memory and spirit will live on. I was never alone and neither are you. God was, is, and always will be at our side, if not carrying us on the toughest of days.

I am thankful for the faith of one child who changed my life and shared Jesus with me. I walked through those doors out of obligation to keep a promise to one boy. I returned home with hope. A hope and relationship to be the catalyst for my life – to live, write, and share Jesus.

My Hope

Since the first Sunday I crossed the threshold at *Community Alliance,* a Christian and Missionary Alliance church – I knew God loved me. I also knew the greatest stress and loss in my life is my sister and the sadness in my parent's eyes during the years that followed.

I can't even imagine the pain they must feel each day, to not know why or where. We all lost Heidi and a part of ourselves that day. I pray daily for God's will for her recovery and for Him to be glorified in the process.

The Lord is my strength and will make my way perfect. He prepares me for the day when Heidi is found. It may not be the outcome I expect or hope for, or pray for, but it is the one God has planned. I need to wait and trust. In God's time we will know. I only pray it is before my parents leave this earth.

Some days are easier than others to talk about Heidi's kidnapping, but with the Lord as my strength I will survive. I can talk with my parents about my concerns, questions, and fears. From exclusion to an active member of the team.

The day Heidi was kidnapped, the abductors took more than her physical body – they took a part of my parents, our community, and me. Because of this, I have spent my adult life feeling like an only child with only memories of being the older of two children.

The Lord opened my ears, eyes, and heart to Him and blesses me each day along the way. He shows me his love and compassion as I become a better wife, mother, daughter and friend. Each day there is a lesson to be learned and blessing to be received.

I may never know where Heidi is, but I know this...God loves all the children. He is omnipresent, everywhere at all times. He lives in my heart, guides my pen, and holds my precious sister in the palm of His hands all at the same time. God didn't take my sister, or yours. He is a loving and merciful God. I continue to pray for the return of our missing loved ones, especially my dear sister.

As I trust, I can face anything the Lord has in store when I let Him lead the way. This book is finished yet there is so much more to share. Our paths separate where my story started. The next step in the process is to forgive.

The sequel to WHERE'S HEIDI? ONE SISTER'S JOURNEY is the journey from anger and frustration to healing and forgiveness, and the journey traveled in the process. We all have someone to forgive. My hope is for the next book to share the possibility of forgiveness, even after tragedy.

We all have someone to forgive. The path we travel to get there will be different yet with God as our compass, we can reach the destination with a renewed heart.

"I waited patiently for the LORD.

He turned to me and heard my cry.

He lifted me out of the slimy pit,

Out of the mud and mire.

He set my feet on a rock

And gave me a firm place to stand."

Psalm 40:1-2

EPILOGUE

Over the years I heard, "I don't know how you or your family can survive after Heidi's kidnapping." My response is usually, "We have to." I realized a lot happened in our life unrelated to Heidi's kidnapping, investigation, and the trials of those charged as I organized my notes for this book.

My purpose for this section of the book is to express it's not only possible but also necessary in order to triumph in spite of your life's tragedy. God is not responsible for my sister's kidnapping. God didn't kill my cousin. He held both of them in His arms. Thank you Jesus.

Each time I added another event or death to my list, grief and amazement overcame me at the same time. I missed my friend's weddings and didn't make it to calling for hours after a friend's loss because I *was* in survival mode. Death and darkness consumed me. "Was" is the key word.

I invited family and friends to help me sift through the jumbled memories with me and this is the best we can do. I apologize if the dates are off a bit, but know they are as close as we can target. I found myself reading the book of Job after putting this together on the computer, go figure.

I am so thankful for the child who proclaimed with boldness, "Mrs. Buske, you need Jesus." He was right. I could not have come through this without God. I pray this book helped you to see the same.

I pray my list helped you to see you too, have a list. Your list will have different years and different events yet we each have one. As you reflect on your list, recognize how each of the things written down had an impact your life and made you the man or woman you are today. Leave the reflection in the mirror and look to the future. You are ready.

The righteous perish,
And no one takes it to heart;
The devout are taken away,
And no one understands
That the righteous are taken away
To be spared from evil.
Those who walk uprightly
Enter into peace;
They find rest as they lie in death.
Isaiah 57:1-2

TIMELINE OF EVENTS

Note: This is to the best of my memory:
Times, dates, and exact details may be incorrect.

1994

April 2	Great Aunt Judy passes away
April 3	Heidi M. Allen is kidnapped
April	My aunt's nephew commits suicide
April 7	Search expert from Texas, USA arrives
April 9	*America's Most Wanted* airs Heidi's story
April 23	Aunt Judy's funeral and burial
April 25	*Day One* airs Heidi's story
April 26	Our Search expert returns to Texas
April 29	I return to work, first time since April 3
May 20	Our Search expert returns to New York
May 25	First arrest in Heidi's case
May 25	Due to my inability to function, left work indefinitely; this is also *National Missing Children's Day*
June 6	Great Aunt Ellen admitted to hospital
June 20	Great Aunt Ellen passes away

June 23/26   Wood stove seized from suspect's home

June 23   Great Aunt Ellen's burial

June   Aunt Nancy Retires due to stress

July   Mrs. "Grandma" Leishman passes away

July 13   Grand Jury, Ed's birthday missed

July 22   A second arrest made in the case with
              an extensive search of his property

July 27   2 cellmate statements released to public

July 29   First indictment made by the grand jury

August 23   Our Search expert returns to New York

September 1   Our Search expert returns to Texas

September 14 Heidi's 19th birthday celebrated

October 12   Arraignment hearing

October 24   Arraignment hearing for 2nd arrested

December 5   A day in court to hear motions

December 8   Another day in court for motions

1995

January 30	Both men return to court, my parents' anniversary is overlooked
January 31	New judge assigned
March 14	A girlfriend to one of the men is arrested and charged with two counts of perjury in connection with Heidi's case
May 8	A little boy and girl from down the road are missing; helicopters are flying overhead to aide in the search
May 22	Pre-trial motions ~ court hearing
May 23	Jury selection begins for one case
May 30	First Trial starts
June 6	Prosecution rest
June	Glenn Federman's song, *Where's Heidi?* released and shared with the family
June 15	Defense rests in case
June 19	Verdict, guilty of 1st degree kidnapping
June 21	Uncle Tom passes away, long illness
June 29	Cousin Shawnacy killed in an accident
June 29	One count of perjury dropped

July 3   The convicted and his girlfriend are wed at the jail with his brother by his side

July   Motions against both cancelled

July 24   Motions cancelled

July 31   Sentencing cancelled

August 7   Convicted brother is sentenced to twenty-five years to life with no eligibility for parole for 25 years

August 13   "Bridge Opening" on County Route 1, the same area Heidi and I frolicked in as children with our friends and family

August 23   Shawnacy's would have been 21 today

September 6   Jury selection, for next brother's case

September 11   Jury selection for the wife (girlfriend)

September 14   Heidi's 20th birthday celebration

September 14   Second court case begins

September 15   The wife's court case begins

September 21   Prosecution rests in brother's case

September 22   Wife's case goes to jury – acquitted

September 27   Defense rests in case against brother

September 28   Closing statements against brother

~ 270 ~

September 29 Second brother's case to jury, acquitted

October 28   "Make a Difference Day" – community
              builds garden in memory of Heidi at the
              intersection of State Route 104 and 104b
              – *Heidi Allen Community Garden*

The most difficult part of this book to write was the last chapter. How do I wrap up a story that will never end? Heidi remains missing, so the search and our hope for answers continue each day.

Even after Heidi is found, the story won't end, similar to when you lose a loved one to death, life is never the same and forever changed and affected.

Will this be the day Heidi is found? There is never closure, as some seem to believe, as it relates to a missing person's case. Closure means something is over; our journey will never be over. We simply transition to the next phase.

The only reason I am able to write this book and share it with you is because of the relationship I have with Jesus Christ. Without God and my faith, I am weak and weary.

My goal was to have my first book reflect the impact God had on my life in a time when I didn't think hope, healing, or joy were possibilities. Yes, those elements are here, but there is more to the story.

There are still difficulties and life tends to feel like a roller coaster ride, but in His strength, I always make it to the end of the ride. At times, my ability to function is mere autopilot. When the adrenaline

~ 273 ~

wears off, Jesus is always there to catch and comfort me. *Why do I try on my own? It is silly.*

My next book will provide more details to my journey since 2004. As with any tragedy, you are not the only one affected – it's okay to feel pain, grief, and anger. You will get through this when you trust God to carry the burden for you. Neither you nor I have the ability to do it ourselves.

Tragedy is sudden and powerful, but one thing we lose sight of in the midst of it is the pain you feel is temporary. I didn't think I could do one more thing or smile one more time.

My Gram told me often, "God won't give you more than you can handle, Lisa. You need to trust Him. His shoulders are bigger." This concept always sounded too simple but she was right, it is simple.

We admit we are sinners, we believe Jesus died on the cross for our sins, and we confess our sins to God. This is between you and Him; if you choose to share with another for accountability, this is a choice, not a necessity.

Once you have done this, invite Jesus to be a part of your life. When you trust God and let Jesus move into your heart, the light will slowly push out the darkness, hurt, and fear.

Remember tears are healing.

"He will wipe every tear from their eyes.

There will be no more death or mourning

Or crying or pain, for the old order

Of things has passed away."

Revelations 21:4

Resource List for Families of Missing Persons

The National Center for Missing and Exploited Children
http://www.missingkids.com/missingkids/servlet/Pub
licHomeServlet?LanguageCountry=en_US
·   **Team Hope**
·   http://www.teamhope.org/

·   **Ride for Missing Children**
·   http://www.therideformissingchildren.com/

The Center for Hope
http://www.hope4themissing.org/
20 Prospect St.
Ballston Spa, NY 12020
518-884-8761
Email: hope4themissing.org

The Surviving Parent's Coalition
http://www.spcoalition.org/

Discussion and Reflection
Turn Your Tragedy to Triumph

To write WHERE'S HEIDI? ONE SISTER'S JOURNEY I had to take a mental and spiritual journey into the past. I didn't travel via time capsule or phone booth but instead through words written in the past and conversations around the kitchen table.

Do you remember that first emotional vomit draft I wrote? I shared this with our women's Bible study group, read a snippet at the *Delta Lake Christian Writers' Gathering*, and then shared it with a few friends. To think I tortured them with such a raw piece of writing is beyond me but I believe it was a necessary step so it could develop into the book you have before you today.

After I shared it during the "Open Mic" at the Delta Conference, the *Wit-n-Wisdom Writers' Group* graciously offered to review and do a minor critique.

Their encouragement, prayers, and honest feedback were enough to move me forward. I thought about putting my manuscript back in the filing cabinet, but God kept nudging me after I learned what I needed to do in order to have a book worth reading.

The original seventy-six page draft illustrated the devastation and hope side by side. The area in need of the most improvement at that time was the amount of information I shared and when. These precious women suggested I add more detail and save my transformation until the end. In order to do this, time travel was necessary and feared.

I lost sleep and the nightmares, years removed, returned. Each newspaper article read or conversation with my family or a friend, helped trigger repressed or forgotten memories, and the memories themselves tormented me once again. Fear, anxiety, stress, and grief returned. I believe this is why the initial draft was vague and resolved the stressors quickly. In hindsight, the best thing I did was deal with the hidden and repressed memories.

My heart still wanted to share hope with you as you read each chapter so this portion of the book came to be. It took a lot of prayer, both my own and from others to conquer the demons of the past. The amount of Scripture I read during the edit and revision phase was double my usual readings.

God has the power and is faithful to help us through the valley (Psalm 23) when we call out to Him. When we seek His help and protection, we need to ask others to join us in the process.

Thanks to God's answering the prayers lifted on my behalf, this book is complete.

Keeping this in mind, I have put together a few questions for you. I encourage you take some time and answer each one with an honest heart. Of course, you can do this in the privacy of your own mind but if you have the opportunity, I pray you would seek a friend, family member, or small group to discuss these questions.

These are similar thoughts, questions, and discussions I experienced myself in order to complete this book. I know it helped me let go of some of my anger, hurt, and resentment. Some of which I believed were already dealt with. I was wrong.

Thank you for reading my book. I pray your heart was touched and you have a different outlook into your life. My Gram told me: "What doesn't kill us makes us stronger." We all have something in life to beat us down. I pray you release the burden to God and move forward a stronger man or woman of God.

With a thankful heart,
Lisa M. Buske

The greatest loss I experienced prior to Heidi's kidnapping related to my ability to have children. I wrote this book from the perspective of one sister after the tragic abduction of her only sister yet this isn't my only tragedy.

If you were to write a book, what would its title be? Why?

In life, we will face various struggles, and sometimes, great tragedy. Our tragedies might be similar or very different. Each person's definition of tragedy is different.

Can you name one tragedy in your life? On a scale of 1 to 10, where does it rank and why? Share this with someone. Remember not to judge another's tragedy, only he or she can determine its severity.

The greatest tragedy I experienced personally was multiple miscarriages, prior to and shortly after Heidi's kidnapping. Then Heidi disappeared. This remains my life's greatest loss and tragedy. Is there one life event that stands out as the worst in your life? Why?

INTRODUCTION

You may not live in the area, or remember Heidi M. Allen's kidnapping on Easter Sunday, April 3, 1994 but I guarantee there is a missing child or person in your area you could name, if not more than one. Where were you when you learned of _____'s disappearance? What were you doing?

I will never forget where I was, or the message that followed when notified of Heidi's kidnapping. The days, months, and years that followed become a hodge-podge of memories. If you are a family member of a missing person (yes, adults go missing too), have you lost precious memories since your loved one's disappearance?

If you aren't directly related to, or connected with a missing person, have you lost a loved one? What are some of your memories?

Think back to your greatest tragedy in life. Do you remember each detail after learning the news or experiencing it first hand? Did you lose track of time and even some memories? Are there some instances that stand out in your mind?

A time to be born, and a time to die...
Ecclesiastes 3:2a

Tragedy is sudden, unexpected, and life changing. Before your life changed forever, before the tragedy happened, and before you questioned "Why?" on a daily basis…what was life like?

My parents lost a daughter. I lost my sister and friend. Ed lost his only sister-in-law. Mags lost the opportunity to meet the aunt who would have spent every waking moment spoiling her. Tragedy does not affect only one person or only you. Who else in your life was affected? How did you support each other?

We can't change the past. Instead, we move forward stronger and more determined. It is the energy and focus as we live that provides opportunity to bless or curse.

How are you channeling your energies? Is there an area you still struggle with that you are willing to share? Have you trusted this to God?

There is a time for everything…
Ecclesiastes 3:1

As you think back to the very moment you learned the news that would change your life forever, do you remember your first thought? Mine was "This has to be a mistake."

Were you able to spring into action and do what needed to be done or did the shock stabilize you? Who was with you? If you could thank them for being there, what would you say?

I found myself lost in thought. It felt as if I was watching a bad movie. My adrenaline ran high and anxiety weakened my knees. I didn't think I could go on but then there were arms wrapped around me. Who held you while you cried? Have you thanked them? It is not too late. If it is easier, write them a note.

If you have done any of these things, will you share with the group as a way to encourage someone else?

...and a season for every activity under heaven:
Ecclesiastes 3:1

CHAPTER 3

The tragic loss of a loved one seems to take your mind back to the last time you saw or talked with them. Heidi and I were the best of friends, with each Thursday spent together as "Sister Day". Regardless of our schedules, we managed to find time for just the two of us.   Memories are precious and no one can take them from you. Embrace them. The first time I spoke to share my testimony and Heidi with the community was a Thursday evening. Only God could have orchestrated this "sister day" for me. When our eyes are open to see His hand at work in our lives, we are blessed.

Did you and your lost loved one have a special day or thing you did together? What was the best day you spent together doing this?

Holidays can be the most difficult days in a year after the loss of a loved one. My least favorite phrase is, "It gets easier." The intentions are honorable yet in my opinion, this is a false statement. It does not get easier but it does become more manageable.

Is there a holiday that is more difficult than others are since the loss of your loved one? Do you have a particular Scripture verse, quote, activity, routine, tradition, or place that eases the pain as you move forward and enjoy life?

Each year on the anniversary of Heidi's kidnapping, April 3, and Easter Sunday, we, as a family, dedicate time to remember her. Heidi was a burst of energy, joy, and love. We know she would not want us to be sad so we choose to do something Heidi enjoyed in her honor. Today, we celebrate the years we had with her instead of mourning the years lost.

Is there something special you do on the anniversary of your loved one's death? Birthday? Family reunions? Holidays? How has this helped you and those around you to heal?

A time to weep...
Ecclesiastes 3:4a

CHAPTER 4

To   wait...doubt...wonder...hope...pray...to
wait alone in the bizarre April rain and snow.
Until I wrote this book, my parents never knew
this. They thought someone was with me. I
thought they knew I was outside waiting for them.
Apologies, forgiveness, and communication
occurred. Take a minute and think about the
initial moments after you lost your loved one. Is
there something that continues to bother you?
Have you thought about sharing this with the
others involved? I encourage you to do so. It
might be uncomfortable at first, but the hurt can't
be healed or the relationship restored until you do.
Your stressor might be a misunderstanding too.

An important aspect in this chapter is prayer.
Although it is not called prayer, I was "talking" to
God. The conversation between God and I was not
holy or beautiful. It was ugly, angry, and at times,
hostile BUT it was between Him and I. Once I
stopped yelling at Him, I was able to listen and let
the healing begin. Can you relate? Will you share
your heart's desire with God?

The first decade following Heidi's kidnapping
I thought God left me and didn't care. It was not
until I started to read my Bible, attend a Bible-

based church, and realized I "needed" Jesus in my life that I was able to look back and see God NEVER left me. I left Him.   The first car to drive by was a Sheriff's. This is not coincidence. I encourage you to remember the moments, days, and years since losing your loved one. Can you recognize any times when you thought you were alone and God didn't care but now that you look back, you realize He never left you?

Evening, morning, and noon
I cry out in distress,
And he hears my voice.
Psalm 55:17

CHAPTER 5

As a family, we have learned the importance of NOT protecting others. I withheld my feelings so I wouldn't burden my parents. The buried hurt built up into layers of darkness on my heart.

My parents withheld their feelings and kept me out of the spotlight to protect me, which I interpreted as "exclusion" instead of protection. Neither of us meant to hurt the other but we had without realizing it. Have you experienced a similar occurrence?

Flashbacks. Since the loss of your loved one, have you found yourself remembering conversations from moments or years prior? At the time, they seemed insignificant but later have a deeper value. I remember Heidi and me talking about Sara Anne Wood.

We couldn't believe something like that would happen to a child so close to us. Our conversation brings tears to my eyes still today. "Lisa, I don't know what I would do if that happened to me."

Was God preparing us? I don't know. All I can say for sure is that this conversation is not forgotten. Is there a flashback you could share?

Another aspect of this chapter is the power of words. The Bible tells us our words have the power to build up or tear down. In the depths of my grief, I suppressed my words with good intentions, as did my parents.

It was the words thought, that tore us down. Once in the open, healing and understanding replaced the hurt.

Have you repressed feelings, avoided conversations, or shut people out in your life with the notion it is best for them? If so, I challenge you to release these feelings, thoughts, and words.

It might not be feasible or possible to share them with the individual but there are options. I wrote letters to people and then burned them. How have you, or can you, let go?

Even though I walk through the valley
of the shadow of death,
I will fear no evil, for you are with me.
Your rod and your staff, they comfort me.
Psalm 23:4

Chapter 6

Tragedy is not new and your particular form of tragedy is not new, until it happens to you. True? Kidnapping was not new when Heidi disappeared, but when my sister disappeared, I had a new perspective on the effect it had on the surviving family and community.

This new perspective is a gift. I am not the only sister searching and Heidi is not the only missing person. I am the only Lisa M. Buske to lose her sister, Heidi M. Allen from Upstate New York. The loss of your loved one is devastating to you and those around you.

We are called to use our pain for something more. How does your new perspective fuel your ambition and joy to help others? What is one way you inspired someone else in a similar situation?

Our stories are not identical because we are all different and unique. You may have lost a loved one to cancer, illness, suicide, an accident, kidnapping, and some I have not listed. While our tragedy is different, one thing is the same. We have all lost someone we love.

I spent years wearing a mask so others would think I was enjoying life, but on the inside I was crumbling. The best thing I did was admit I couldn't do it anymore on my own. No more masks, just the grieving heart searching for joy. I found mine in a relationship with Jesus.

The first step is to remove the mask and let the healing begin. Was it difficult to admit your pain? Is there a particular Scripture verse you clung to?

If you read this book with a broken and empty heart, are you able to see there is hope encompassed around you? God is waiting and ready to listen, all you need to do is open the door.

Find a friend, relative, or a member of the clergy to pray with and for you. If you read this book with a friend in mind, have you shared with them? Is there a way you could reach out to them today that might help peel back the mask?

Praise be to the God and
Father of our Lord Jesus Christ,
The Father of compassion and the God of all comfort...
2 Corinthians 1:3

Change is usually a dreaded word yet for the families of a missing person, it is a blessing. Compassionate Heroes Accelerating Needed Growth for Everyone's missing child. Change is necessary. Word of Heidi's kidnapping, her photograph, and even flyers spread within hours. Today, this happens within minutes.

Each day there is change with our technology. I choose to embrace it. Children are being found, cold cases solved, and awareness taught because of CHANGE. Do you remember a time before cellular phones and the Internet? What is your favorite technological advance? Your least? Why?

Teamwork is vital to the success of any mission. Our community rallied to find Heidi. Easter dinners got cold. Easter dresses and suits were replaced with clothes appropriate for searching. My parents lost one of their daughters, and the community lost one of their own. After the loss of your loved one, how did your family, friends, and possibly community rally to help you?

A common theme associated with Heidi's case and search combined with the continued support from family, friends, community, and now readers is this....Thanks.

My parents, Ed, Mags, and I do not know how to express the magnitude of thanks we have for each of you in those first days until today. We appreciate you. Although only two small words, they come from our hearts...Thank you. Whom do you need to thank today?

I wait for the LORD, my whole being waits,
And in his word I put my hope.
I wait for the Lord
More than watchmen wait for the morning,
More than watchmen wait for the morning.
Psalm 130:5-6

CHAPTER 8

Every second matters. We do not know what might happen after we blink our eyes. One moment Heidi was cashing out a customer and the next, she was missing.

While I slept, Heidi fought for her life. As people drove by, Heidi was fighting for her life. Do you understand the value in one minute? Is there someone you should call right now so they know you love them?

As with most tragedy, there has to be a neutral area for families and friends to gather. After Heidi's kidnapping, the Fire Department's banquet hall became this place.

Outside of Heidi's disappearance, our meeting place was usually my Gram and Aunt Nancy's home. Where do you go when life's tragedies come? Why is this a place of healing and security?

Tragedy and grief have such power on one's mind, physical and spiritual state. I know I was alive and active but there are months and portions of the years following Heidi's kidnapping I have lost forever. Friends got married, neighbors passed away, and I even attended some of these events with no memory of being there. I learned a valuable lesson through this.

Grief, pain, anger, and the range of negative (and normal) emotions associated with tragedy have the potential to put us in survival mode. Since preserving a memory is not our focus, they are either repressed or forgotten. In my case, I lost years of time and memories.

Thanks to notes, articles, friends, and family I was able to regain some. If you experienced a similar loss of memories, were you able to restore any? How?

Do nothing out of selfish ambition or vain conceit.
Rather, in humility value others above yourselves,
Not looking to your own interests but
Each of you to the interests of the others.
Philippians 2:3-4

CHAPTER 9

Although our community and law enforcement had never led and operated a search and rescue effort for a missing person, they excelled. It was an organized chaos with many working together with one common goal, to find Heidi. In your life's tragedy, how did your team pull together to accomplish necessary tasks?

Compassion or Exclusion? I wanted to help but wasn't allowed to. Volunteers said, "Lisa, have a seat. What do you need honey? Are you okay? Have a seat. We will get you whatever you need", but I heard, "Go to your corner, Lisa. Bad Lisa."

Looking back, I understand and appreciate their compassion and concern for me. I could not have done the things I offered to do but didn't realize how incapable I was at the time.

Have you offered compassion only to have it received differently? Did you find yourself in my position? What could someone have said or done differently that would have been encouragement?

In truth, all I wanted to do was curl up into the fetal position and cry until the tears stopped, but this was not an option. I gained thirty pounds in the first month after my sister's kidnapping.

I shut the world out and lived in a fog. In those first weeks, I never succumbed to my desire of a gut-wrenching cry fest but maybe it would have helped me to let go of the pain earlier.

After the loss of your loved one, did you cry and give it to God or hold it in for the sake of others? How did it feel when you finally let it all go?

The LORD hears his people when
they call to him for help.
He rescues them from all their troubles.
The LORD is close to the brokenhearted.
He rescues those whose spirits are crushed.
The righteous person faces many troubles,
but the LORD comes to the rescue each time.
Psalm 34:17 – 19

Shocking statements paralyze your capacity to think and sometimes, to live without fear. Is there a sentence or question that stands out in your mind after your loss? You know one of those 'did he or she seriously just ask or say that?' instances.

When the officer told me, "Most criminals return to the scene of the crime. It gives them a thrill", I could have vomited. How would you respond? I was in disbelief and prayed it wasn't true.

To look back is such a gift. My thought process and ability to make educated decisions was held captive by the grief. I am thankful for honest answers, helpful volunteers, and the many prayer warriors at work in New Haven and beyond when I was rendered helpless.

When you look back, is there an instance when you were told no or didn't get your way that you are thankful for now?

We all need someone to hold us when we fall. God is there. We need to feel His love through the arms of another is powerful. I don't remember who held me the first time I opened the floodgates. I appreciate their love and silence. Who held you when you cried?

The LORD is close to the brokenhearted
and saves those who are crushed in spirit.
Psalm 34:18

~ 305 ~

CHAPTER 11

Oh my gosh, the "What if?" questions in life. Sad to say, these are not limited to tragedy. As humans, we tend to question God when we don't get what we want or when things don't turn out as we'd planned.

It took me awhile to realize the "What if?"s were stifling me and preventing complete healing. Instead of "What if?" we need to ask, "What's next?" Have you ever asked yourself, "What if?"

How did these two little words hold you back? If you were to ask, "What's next?" how could this change your perspective on life?

The pain felt after the loss of your loved one can't compare, but sometimes when you look into the eyes of another, your pain takes a back seat as you mourn their loss instead.

The worst look I have seen is the empty, depressed, and hopeless look embedded into the depths of my parents' eyes after they lost Heidi.

Who else affected by the same tragedy you experienced was able to capture your attention enough to shift your focus off yourself, and onto another?

We lacked for nothing after Heidi's kidnapping. Our community searched, cooked, baked, organized, copied, lead, and prayed, among other things.

Tragedy is devastating. It seems to rally families and sometimes, entire communities together for the better good of the situation. What memories of unity or teamwork stand out in your mind from your life's tragedy?

You hear, O LORD the desire of the afflicted.
You encourage them, and you listen to their cry…
Psalm 10:17

Tragedy and grief take your mind captive while igniting a physical depletion if allowed. This was a struggle for me because I didn't have something to focus on or lean on for strength. If we don't have something to hope in, it is difficult to maintain yourself.

Logical thinking smothered by the pain. Without a faith in God, I am not sure how any of us got through it. Thankfully, God loves us and never gives up on His people.

Were you able to keep it together and assume the leadership role, or did you struggle to get dressed in the morning? If you are the leader, when did you realize you needed a break? If you are the struggler, when did you realize you needed help?

Although consumed by grief, I tried to hide it from my parents and others. I thought I was successful until I overheard a conversation between my parents. It was at this moment I realized the only person I was fooling was myself.

Can you think of a time when you thought you had it all together and no one knew stress was beating you down, and then someone who cared for you mentioned it to you? Have you thanked them for saving you from further exhaustion or depression?

At the time of Heidi's disappearance, it felt as if the world had stopped. I couldn't leave the center and had no desire to do so either. It took my parents forcing me to go home for a nap and shower to leave. It was the quickest nap and shower I ever took.

Fear and wonder captivated me. I forgot others were still going to work, raising families, and carrying out daily activities. My only thought was, "What if they find Heidi and I am not here? She will think I don't care or love her." Of course this an irrational thought.

Did you have moments of irrational thoughts in the midst of your tragedy? Who or what helped you snap back into reality? Someone else we need to thank.

My soul is in anguish.
How long, O LORD, how long?
Psalm 6:3

CHAPTER 13

Due to the nature of my life's tragedy, a kidnapping, press conferences and media attention became part of our life. Our family was on display around the clock. Each facial expression, hug, or conversation captured on someone's camera or video camera, "just in case" it would be a breaking news story.

Sadly, tragedy points a spotlight on the suffering family. You may not have experienced a media spotlight but I guarantee you all gathered at someone's home or even church. The grieving person seems to be center stage with others positioned around them.

Where did your family gather? Where did you escape for a few minutes of solitude? How did you spend those precious "alone" moments?

Stress affects people differently. I like to be busy, which I have learned is an avoidance tactic. (I know, Ouch!) It is true though. My pastor challenged me after a session, "Lisa, why do you stay so busy? Why don't you like the quiet?"

I didn't know how to answer those questions then, but thankfully I can today. I won't claim to have it all together but I am learning. Life is a process. Since then I try to keep my focus on God and seek His strength as I listen for direction instead of surrounding myself with busyness.

I will pose these same questions to you – Why do you stay so busy, especially in the midst of a tragedy?

The result of stress and tragedy is the same regardless of the form in which it enters our life. It is called exhaustion. After Heidi disappeared we would not, and could not, stop until she was found.

Our human bodies can only take so much before they collapse. We need to know when it is time to ask for help. Who did or could you ask? First God, then ____?

...but we also rejoice in our sufferings because we know
That suffering produces perseverance;
Perseverance, character; and character, hope.
And hope does not disappoint us,
Because God has poured out his love
Into our hearts by the Holy Spirit,
Whom he has given us.
Romans 5:3-5

CHAPTER 14

Tragedy takes its toll on you physically, mentally, and spiritually. Less than forty-eight hours into the search, we recognized we needed more help. Mom and Dad tried to do it all but this isn't realistic.

Thanks to my Aunt and Unc, help arrived to manage and lead our team of volunteers so my parents could rest. How long did it take you to realize you needed help and couldn't do it on your own? Whom did you call?

We can't and should not try to get through life's challenges on our own. This was my biggest mistake and hardest lesson to learn. My hope for this book is for others not to spend ten years searching and learning the hard way.

We brought in an expert from Texas to lead the search but what we need as individuals is to bring The Expert, God, into our lives and heart. Can you remember the first prayer you lifted to God after the news of your loved one's passing?

Our Texan-twist shared his expertise to search and find with one goal in mind, to find Heidi. God shares similar things with us through the Bible, but His goal is broader. He seeks to save the lost. I was lost, but thanks to one child, I found God.

Do you believe in God? Did you believe in God but stopped after the tragedy? If you believe in God, do you have a relationship with Jesus? Is this something you desire? Whom can you call to share this with?

Come to me, all you who are weary and burdened,
And I will give you rest.
Take my yoke upon you and learn from me,
For I am gentle and humble in heart,
And you will find rest for your souls.
Matthew 11:28 – 29

CHAPTER 15

Introductions are important and the first step to forming a relationship. When Rick arrived his intentions were to find Heidi, not make friends. He still prioritized meeting the community. Why? Because he knew it is through relationships that he would learn.

He learned about the search, Heidi, family dynamics, the community, and so many other things. He then designed all this into his search and rescue efforts. My opinion was both pro and con, my emotions were still riding the roller coaster, and my body decided it was okay to sleep.

When did you accept that it was okay to rest? What happened or would need to happen to let you rest?

We revisit change again in this chapter. Compassionate Heroes Accelerating Needed Growth for Everyone's missing child ~ Rick came in and freed my parents from the burden of leadership and management so they could focus on Heidi.

The exclusion hurt and was necessary. In hindsight I recognize this. Was there a time you looked back and said, "Thank goodness 'person'

~ 314 ~

did "action", I don't know what I would have done without him or her." Did you realize the impact their one action would have on your life?

The statement, "Business isn't personal, it's purposeful", brought a slew of emotions that I was not prepared for. Eighteen years later, I understand why and the importance of this being the center's mission. It is difficult to make administrative decisions when family is involved.

We needed to focus on finding Heidi. This was our purpose. What is your purpose? Are you asking yourself, "On what level?" Good. When you lost your loved one, what was your purpose? What is it today? How has it changed?

A time to tear down...
Ecclesiastes 3:3b

CHAPTER 16

It is a struggle to remain hopeful after a tragedy. If you are waiting for, "If you believe in God, have a relationship with Jesus, and read your Bible every day, then life will be nothing but wonderful", then you will be waiting a long time.

These things don't eliminate the pain or save you from life's trials and troubles, BUT they will provide you with the strength, wisdom, and guidance you'll need for the journey.

I didn't have any of these when Heidi disappeared, making it difficult for ME to do it. That is the key though, WE can't do this on our own and God doesn't want us to.

Think about a time when you trusted God to get you through a tough time and a time you tried to do it on your own. What is the difference? Which would you recommend?

One of my favorite phrases in this book is "vigilantes to experts" because of the beauty in the transformation. I do not know if cities work the same way but in our little town, neighbors still watch out for each other and their families.

My parents lost their youngest daughter but an entire community lost their Heidi. They searched with their hearts on their sleeve. Rick's addition and leadership to the team provided the necessary discipline, training, and relationship required.

God offers us the same guidance so we can transition from vigilante citizens to eternal experts and share His love with others. A vigilante is the best witness of God's transformational power. Is there a vigilante in your life that you have watched blossom into an expert?

With your "vigilante to expert" person in mind, how have they influenced your life and the lives of others? Do they recognize the change they are portraying?

Have you told them? Sometimes the vigilante expert can't see his or her self as anything more than a vigilante until someone notices they have changed.

Please understand a "vigilante expert" is not perfect. There was only one perfect man, Jesus, the Bible calls us to be like Him.

Carry each other's burdens,
And in this way you will fulfill the law of Christ.
Galatians 6:2

Tough decisions are necessary in life. They help to make us wiser, more thoughtful, and educated. Sometimes though, the right decision is the most heart breaking to make. We use logic and reasoning and realize we need to trump the desire of our heart. The goal was to search until we found Heidi but the reality was volunteers were dwindling and needs were intensifying.

This was probably the most difficult decision my parents and the sheriff had to make up until this point. They did what was right for the sake of our wonderful volunteers. We couldn't sacrifice families, health, and morale.

Have you experienced a time when a difficult decision needed to be made? How did the logic and reason compare to your heart's desire? Which won?

Reinforcements arrived to provide necessary help. Everyone has a role to play and job to do. Typically when a loved one passes away there are certain things to be done and everyone works together to ensure it is all done within the short time frame.

Sometimes though, regardless of how many people are available, you need to ask for help from outside the family. The beautiful part of loss and tragedy is the teamwork birthed from the discourse.

Is there a person, family, church, or organization that comes to mind when you think of the people who stepped in when you couldn't do anymore? Have you been on the giving end? Whether you gave or received, or both, how did you feel at the time?

Search teams scoured fields, woods, and roadsides for the smallest of clues. To hear "We found a white canvas sneaker" brought hope until we learned it was a men's size eleven. Ugh.

The words expressed through song, notes, cards, posters, and conversation burst with love, compassion, and encouragement. An angel sits on my bookshelf. Handmade cards tucked into bins. Posters made by children.

All of these are small symbols of hope. Is there an item or act of kindness that stands out in your mind? Why?

Who of you by worrying can
Add a single hour to your life?
Luke 12:25

What is my purpose? A question I asked myself daily after Heidi disappeared. Everyone had an assignment, task, or an errand to do. It felt as if everyone participated but me. It is vital everyone involved knows he or she are important and have a role to play, especially in times of trauma. My parents, family, and volunteers constantly checked on me. I didn't feel like anyone trusted me enough to give me a job. I needed a purpose. Once I had one, my outlook brightened a bit. When did you feel the most purposeful? Was there someone or something that initiated this? Were you able to encourage someone else?

Good intentions gone badly, is an understatement. The majority of our family and extended family resided at the command center but my Gram remained home. She cooked, baked, and cleaned to keep busy.

In her mission to keep busy she cleaned Heidi's room upstairs so the investigators would not think she was messy. She washed all the laundry, dusted, and even changed the sheets. Heidi's room had never been so clean.

Along with dust, Gram inadvertently erased any DNA and scent of Heidi that might have been available. A genuine gesture of love turned into one of Gram's greatest regrets. Her tears and sorrow were so great, it still hurts to think of it today. No one blamed her, she never forgave herself. A lesson learned.

Is there a time in your life you meant to help but in the end regretted your actions? Why?

I met many people in a short time during the search efforts. Some were volunteers, law enforcement, or professional search teams (only to name a few), and to remember everyone I met would be impossible. When I returned to church, one woman seemed familiar. I couldn't place her.

In God's time I realized she was one of the searchers with the dog teams. I was overwhelmed and didn't know what to say so I started with, "I remember".

Is there a time you recognize someone but can't put a name to his or her face? Once you realize how you know them, how does it make you feel?

A time to search...
Ecclesiastes 3:6a

CHAPTER 19

Candlelight vigils became a part of our lives after Heidi's kidnapping. It was a way the community could come together to mourn and pray. I didn't quite grasp the concept at the time and was always amazed at the number of people who gathered in the yard next to the fire hall each evening.

Today, I know the power of prayer, and God's people coming together in prayer are the first and most important thing we can do. Thank goodness God placed some angels in our path to organize these events. Have you ever attended a candlelight vigil? Why did you prioritize this event above others?

My memories are few and scattered for a couple of years after losing Heidi. Some are fuzzy and others are clear. I cherish most of my clear memories while others can still haunt my sleep if I am not conscious to pray them away.

I remember a few hugs, Ret and Lisa driving me home to gather more pictures of Heidi, Heidi's high school volleyball team showing up to do the Hokey Pokey in her honor, and wax burning my hand at the first candlelight vigil. I also remember some horrible things.

Smells, songs, a phrase, or an old rerun on television trigger the memories. Some are new each time I remember. Is this God's way of protecting me? I don't know. What has triggered a memory of your loved one or the last time you saw or talked with them?

Heidi's kidnapping affected our entire family, community, and neighboring communities. Tragedy is not isolated to one person and can have a butterfly effect.

How can we ensure our actions create positive effects and strengthen instead of being negative? The time spent with our community, restored relationships, created new ones, and made us even stronger. A blessing in the midst of tragedy.

What blessings do you see because of your tragedy?

Be devoted to one another in love.
Honor one another above yourselves.
Never be lacking in zeal, but keep your spiritual fervor,
serving the Lord. Be joyful in hope,
Patient in affliction, faithful in prayer.
Share with the Lord's people who are in need.
Practice hospitality.
Romans 12:9-13

The joy and hope associated with the candlelight vigils blow out as quickly as my temper ignited. I attended the vigils but not for the right reasons. I only went because it was the right thing to do, not because I believed it would bring Heidi home.

Did you do or say things because you believed this is what people wanted to see and hear? If so, when did you started to respond honestly?

"I left the vigil bitter and hurt. Excluded and separated from my parents and sister once again. I spewed words of anger and frustration the entire way home. Thank goodness, only Ed came with me as projectile emotional vomit to God left my heart through my mouth, the entire mile back home. I don't want anything to do with God.

I not only walked away from my family and the community that day, I turned my back and walked away from God."

If you believed in God, did you hold fast to your faith when life got hard? If your faith resembled mine, who or what did you use as a scapegoat?

I spent years angry and holding a grudge toward this innocent pastor. As you learned later in the story, I wrote her a letter to confess my hurt and anger, and she in turn apologized to me.

Only God could have orchestrated such grace to me. Do you have a story of "Only God could..." to share?

For our struggle is not against flesh and blood,
But against the rulers,
Against the authorities,
Against the powers of this dark world
And against the spiritual forces
Of evil in the heavenly realms.
Ephesians 6:12

CHAPTER 21

The story I don't dwell on in this book is some people's greatest interest: the case. As the sister of a missing person I recognize this is newsworthy to some, but for us, the case relives the tragedy. An arrest without answers as to where Heidi is, is painful and held me captive for years.

Is there an aspect of your life's tragedy considered newsworthy to others, but tears you apart on the inside? How do you handle moments like this?

If allowed, tragedy will hold you hostage. I was afraid to leave New Haven because "something might happen" or "news might break". But this is not realistic or healthy.

Thankfully, my husband and parents forced me to get away for a time of relaxation. Were you able to separate yourself from the situation and take a needed break of restoration? Or did you need a loving nudge from friends and family?

As we spent the weekend traveling in Toronto, there was a pattern. I would start to relax and enjoy myself and then feel guilty for the simple pleasures. My rationale was: "We don't know where Heidi is. She is being tortured or is dead and I am here laughing and having fun."

Guilt is another of satan's weapons used against us. It took a long time for me to realize I could and should enjoy life, if for no other reason than Heidi would not want me depressed and secluded.

If you struggled with guilt, how did you overcome it?

Be still before the LORD
And wait patiently for him;
Do not fret when people succeed in their ways,
When they carry out their wicked schemes.
Psalm 37:7

CHAPTER 22

A common theme that prevented us from traveling much is the "If we leave, something will happen" mentality. I struggled with this for nearly a decade. To learn of another arrest when we are hours away and in another country was the foundation for this false thought process.

Is there an event from your life's tragedy that caused a similar reaction? How did you overcome this irrational thought process? Mine required prayer and trust.

"I clung to the news article as if it were my life force until I reached my parents' house." Instead of clinging to God, I held onto the newspaper. Whom did you cling to?

Heidi was loved by our community and still is today. We are grateful, appreciative, and blessed by this love. Although a blessing, it can be difficult at times. After the arrests and the publication of the cellmate's descriptive statements, it was a challenge to even go to the grocery store.

Have you ever stood in the grocery store and listened to someone talk about how your sister was murdered? I have. Have you sat at lunch with the topic of discussion being the newest kidnapping case on the news? I have. I must admit I might be guilty of talking about a news story that is your tragedy when you were in the line with me too. If I have, I apologize. Headlines generate conversations. No one is malicious in his or her discussions but news is just that, news.

What would your headline look like if it were on the front page? How would you feel if your greatest pain was discussed while selecting the perfect melon?

A time to tear…
Ecclesiastes 3:7a

CHAPTER 23

Twelve years after Heidi's disappearance I asked the pastor if we could have a prayer service for Heidi at the church. He said yes. I was nervous but felt God was calling me to do this. I was nervous to share my heart's prayer but felt at peace about doing it.

"The hours, tears, and edits involved to put together a three minute prayer exhausted me." God used my preparation to convict me of my wrong as it pertained to the precious pastor I spent years blaming. I had to apologize. Until I wrote the letter, she never knew. Her forgiveness was a relief and blessing.

If you have negative feelings toward another and feel bad about it then I challenge you to express them and ask for forgiveness. The rest is in God's hands.

You never know the lives God will touch through your life's tragedy. Although the tragedy is terrible and devastating, God can use all things for good. Suzie created and dedicated a video documentary to Heidi and her kidnapping.

My mother joined Suzie in her class for the premiere. It was a difficult day for both of them.

Their mutual love for Heidi allowed them an opportunity to share Heidi with others, mourn, and heal all at the same time.

Is there a friend of your loved one who honored your loved one in such a way you were blessed?

The community continues to show their support and love. A physical way was the Heidi Allen Memorial Garden located at the intersection where she was last seen. It is in the shape of a star.

At the dedication, someone read the reason for the star, but this is one of those lost memories. Is there a way you and your family or community remember your lost loved one?

"You turned my wailing into dancing.
you removed my sackcloth and clothed me with joy,
that my heart may sing to you and not be silent.
Lord my God, I will give you thanks forever."
Psalm 30: 11 – 12

Prayer is simply talking to God. Why is prayer such a scary concept to us? I wonder if it is because we know God is faithful to answer. As if the notion to pray isn't a stretch, to pray aloud was even more difficult. When I finished, it was the most healing.

"The first of many public prayers, it is joyful to remember Heidi in prayer instead of searching the woods." Are you comfortable sharing your prayers with others? To pray aloud?

An important note about this first prayer: it was written and prayed in 2006. This is not the prayer I would lift to Heaven today, but it was the one in my heart at the time. I didn't change it to correct theology or grammar but left it exactly the way it is.

A couple of friends who helped with the editing pointed out some of this but I decided to leave it as it is so you can see that this is a process. I didn't say, "I believe in Jesus" one minute and become who I am overnight. And prayerfully I will be stronger and different by the time this book is released.

Are you familiar with the phrase "life-long learner"? This is the mentality required to live a life of faith. Are you ready to start the journey?

"I am living proof it is possible to change when you have faith in Jesus. It is a change from the inside out. As I asked God to bring Heidi home, I knew he would answer.

He always answers prayer. Whether it be a yes, no, or not right now. He is faithful and does answer. I will wait." Are you ready to change?

A time to speak...
Ecclesiastes 3:7b

CHAPTER 25

Death versus disappearance is a topic many don't think of. I struggled for years to accept that Heidi is most likely dead. There is always that smidgen of hope she might be alive somewhere.

When a loved one passes away, we say "good-bye" and then join our family for the burial. But with a missing person, what do you do? Do you buy a headstone and cemetery plot? Will others think you gave up if you do?

What if your missing loved one is found, will they be angry and think you gave up? I don't know the answers but know it is different than knowing your loved one has died. Do you buy the headstone? Why or why not?

My Gram Mary told me, "Parents shouldn't have to watch their children die. It is the worst pain a mother or father can face." I will add, it was the worst pain a grandparent could bear too. Not only did she lose one granddaughter at a young age, she lost two in just over a year. How does she survive? ...Prayer.

What role does prayer have in your life? Is it a lifeline or last resort?

My Gram's statement, "Just pray", is how she felt. In truth, prayer is the first thing we should do. Gram had it right. A dear friend of mine does not believe we "just" pray because it is the very thing God has called us to do. We should say, "We can pray." Do you pray or "just" pray?

This is the confidence we have in approaching God:
That if we ask anything according to his will,
He hears us.
And if we know that he hears us –
Whatever we ask –
We know that we have what we asked of him.
1 John 5:14-15

Have you ever sat bedside to a dying loved one? I have. I have family and friends who will not visit when life is this close to ending, but I cherish these last moments. My sister and family were deprived of these moments.

Instead of having someone to hold her hand, wipe the sweat from her brow, or tell her it would be okay…she endured horrors we can't imagine. I wonder if this is why I cherish these last moments.

When a loved one is passing away and the doctor says, "Call in the family", are you the first one there or the one at home praying, baking, and preparing? I don't believe one is right or wrong but I chose to be there, it is a gift of time and good-byes.

As my aunt neared the end of her battle with cancer, she kept her eyes fixed on Jesus. Would you be able to respond in the same way? "She smiles. 'No. Do not cry. I am going to be okay. I know where I am going.'

'I know but I'll still miss you. I just …'

'Lisa, in a little while, I will know where Heidi is. I'm okay.'"

"A sister-in-Christ once told me, 'Treat Jesus like you do your best friends.'" Ouch! Would you cancel on a friend because you are busy, tired, or just plain lazy? No. We need to honor God the same way.

Think of it as the like the first VBS song you learned, "What a friend we have in Jesus". How are you treating your most faithful and true friend?

Blessed is the man who listens to me,
Watching daily at my doors,
Waiting at my doorway.
For whoever finds me finds life
And receives favor from the LORD.
Proverbs 8:34 – 35

CHAPTER 27

To remember a missing loved one is different because we don't know if they are alive or dead. At the first anniversary of Heidi's kidnapping, I locked myself in my house with all the curtains and doors shut. "I remain in my pajamas and in bed. Ed puts in an old home movie of Heidi and me. I lay in bed to cry – all day." A routine I carried on for years.

Instead of seeking the support of God or others, I hid in the dark. Nothing good ever comes from the dark. If you hid like me, did you ever emerge from the darkness happier? I didn't.

Eventually, the darkness won and I started to seek help from psychics and others claiming to "know" where Heidi was. They even claimed they could talk to her. Oh my goodness, I can't begin to tell you the amount of time, money, and tears wasted on these lies.

I left the confines of my dark bedroom only to surround myself with darkness until it consumed me. The Wiccan minister always opened in a prayer and closed with, "In Jesus' Name", so I thought she was legit.

The more I read my Bible, the more I can see this is Satan's trickery. I should have known it was wrong when I couldn't tell my aunts about it. Hmm, hidden. What are you hiding? Who are you listening to? Is it of God or one of satan's lies?

Eventually God reveals the lies but then I couldn't trust God or the psychics. I didn't know what to do so I went back to school to complete my degree. Always busy, never dealing. God used my new training to introduce me to the child who would change my life.

"A career didn't change me, the children and the friendships with the teachers did. God used the students and my colleagues at New Haven Elementary to open my heart to grieve, heal, and invite Jesus back in to my life."

What or who brought you to Jesus?

Do not turn to mediums or seek out spiritists,
For you will be defiled by them.
I am the LORD your God.
Leviticus 19:31

Chapter 28

I believe many adults tried to express the same words as the one child who changed my life. Gram told me all the time, "Give it to God." My aunt said, "Trust God." And some told me to "Invite Jesus to live in your heart." That one just scared me, but when a child looked me in the eyes with such determination, love, and concern and said, "Mrs. Buske, you need Jesus."

Has anyone told you any of these statements? Did one affect you more than the other? Have you said yes? I didn't think I needed Jesus, but I did. And so do you.

"I walked out the door of the Community Alliance Church in New Haven, overwhelmed and hopeful." Overwhelmed was a familiar feeling but to be hopeful, this was new.

Have you been to church since your life's tragedy? Why or why not? Do you have a friend or family member praying you will join them this Sunday? Call them.

"I do not remember the exact Sunday I accepted Christ in my heart but I will never forget the young man God used to tell me, 'Mrs. Buske, you need Jesus.' He was so right." Some know specific details pertaining to the day they invited Jesus into their life. I can't think of one particular day. I know it was a communion Sunday, but other than that, all I know is the healing began the first day I walked into the church because of a promise.

If you have accepted Jesus, have you shared you shared your testimony? If you do not have a relationship with Jesus yet and it is something you want to learn more about, ask the friend or family member you know is praying for you. They will hold you while you cry and Jesus will wipe the tears.

"He reached down from on high and took hold of me.
He drew me out of deep waters.
He rescued me from my powerful enemy,
From my foes, who were too strong for me.
They confronted me in the day of my disaster,
But the Lord was my support.
He brought me out into a spacious place.
He rescued me because he delighted in me."
Psalms 18:16 – 19

In the case of kidnapping, there are multiple organizations and families available to help. Their missions focus on the missing.

If you have lost a loved one to disease, cancer, tragedy, or suicide, then there are probably organizations and support groups out there for you too. Have you connected with any of the organizations specializing in your need?

Another aspect of these organizations is your involvement with them. There are various levels of involvement just like there are various stages in the grieving process. I don't think this is a coincidence.

My first *Ride for Missing Children*, I watched in amazement. My first trip to Albany for *Missing Person's day* left me reflective. Each year I am able to do more.

As I trust God, I continue to do more. With God, you can move forward too. Have you tried?

We need like-minded people in our lives to help us understand we are not alone. Of course, God is first, until I met Sandy, I felt like no one understood how I felt or understood the pain I experienced.

Is there someone in a similar situation you could talk to?

What does the worker gain from his toil?
Ecclesiastes 3:9

CHAPTER 30

The National Center for Missing and Exploited Children is one amazing organization, to say the least. You might be more familiar with the production of missing person fliers but there is so much more to them. They are constantly in schools, businesses, and communities to increase awareness. They have different outreaches and area offices. It only takes one poster to be seen by the right person to bring a missing child home.

Did you know one poster makes a difference?

"I encourage my daughter daily to be the best she can be, to trust God, and lean not on her own understanding. (Prov. 3:5) As she watches the rider's dedication and love for missing and exploited children, she always cries.

Each time she watches the riders interact with the students at the school stops she smiles and says, "I want to be like them when I grow up Mom. Kids need good role models." Are you that role model? Who is your child's role model?

"If someone suggested I speak and write about my story in 1994, I would have laughed it off. But today, I look forward to the people I will meet and pray to be the best writer, speaker, and person I can be – sharing hope with other siblings and those affected by kidnapping."

With God, you never know. Will you trust Him with your life and to help you do things you never dreamed?

The LORD your God is with you,
The Mighty Warrior who saves.
He will take great delight in you.
In his love he will longer rebuke you,
But will rejoice over you with singing.
Zephaniah 3:17

Chapter 31

This was the most difficult chapter to write. My precious sister remains missing. We continue to search, hope, and pray for her return and answers. Each day in the life of a missing person's family is a journey. Our lives are forever changed.

An example of this is the effect of news broadcast that start with "Body Found" or "Cold Case Solved". How do you respond when you see this headline? To the family of a missing child, we are instantaneously, back to the day we lost our loved one. I have been in the grocery store, volunteering in the Music Booster's fundraising tent, and at work when the news hits the public.

My stomach tightens, my hands shake, and I start praying. Do I pray for it to be Heidi or do I pray it isn't Heidi so there is still hope she might be alive? Then there is guilt for not knowing how to pray so I pray to accept whatever God reveals.

Whether a loved one has been gone one day or multiple decades, the pain doesn't go away and the media's ability to take your mind captive doesn't go away.

What has the ability to take your mind captive and return you to the moment tragedy struck? How do you deal with it?

In the beginning I said you had a story to tell. Do you see your story now? How does your story end? Or do you have new chapters to write? Is it like mine with an open ending, or do you know how to close it now? I pray these questions helped you to see there is hope and healing.

You are stronger today than you were yesterday. Congratulations!

The next time life's stressors come your way, how will you respond? Do you have a new outlook? Will you pray first?

I have a sequel in mind for this book on forgiveness. I think this is the next step. What about you?

I waited patiently for the LORD.
He turned to me and heard my cry.
He lifted me out of the slimy pit,
Out of the mud and mire.
He set my feet on a rock
And game me a firm place to stand.
Psalm 40:1-2

ABOUT THE AUTHOR

Lisa M. Buske's sister, Heidi M. Allen was kidnapped on April 3, 1994, never to be seen or heard from again. God has taken a tragic instance of her life and transformed it into a life-saving occurrence.

She writes with passion and out of obedience for the God who saved her knowing others needed to hear her story. Lisa's relationship with Jesus opened the door to a hope and healing she didn't think was possible.

Her life proves it is possible to survive when God is part of the equation. Lisa's husband Ed, daughter, Mary and her parents serve as Lisa's team as she writes and speaks. Lisa's faith in God and dedication to family motivate and inspire her to do and be the best woman, wife, mother, and sister she can be.

OTHER BOOKS BY LISA M. BUSKE:
When the Waves Subside – There is Hope

TO LEARN MORE ABOUT LISA M. BUSKE:
Website: http://LisaMBuske.com
Blog: http://www.lisambuske.com/blog.html
Twitter: @LisaBuske

TO SEND LISA M BUSKE A NOTE:
Lisa M Buske
P.O. Box 261
New Haven, New York 13121

Praise be to the God and Father

Of our Lord Jesus Christ,

The Father of compassion

And the God of all comfort,

Who comforts us

In all our troubles?

So that we can comfort

Those in any trouble

With the comfort we ourselves

Have received from God.

2 Corinthians 1:3-4

A Place To Jot Your Thoughts

Made in the USA
Middletown, DE
29 January 2020